LOCOMOTION PAPERS E. MASON,

The
Glencorse Branch

by
Jeff Hurst

THE OAKWOOD PRESS

British Library Cataloguing in Publication Data
A Record for this book is available from the British Library
ISBN 0 85361 539 X

Typeset by Oakwood Graphics.
Repro by Ford Graphics, Ringwood, Hants.
Printed by The Witney Press, Witney, Oxon.

**For Margaret, Jennifer and Laura,
for their patience and understanding.**

The branch goods pauses at Glencorse, on a sunny day sometime before World War II. The lack of traffic at this period is apparent from the single van making up the train.
J.L. Stevenson Collection

Title page: The Stephenson Locomotive Society special, which was run on 25th April, 1951, made a stop on Glencorse viaduct. Here the crew of 'D34' class 4-4-0 No. 62471 *Glen Falloch* pose for their photograph, with driver J. 'Stonewall' Jackson on the right, and fireman A. Oog *(centre)*. *R.W. Lynn Collection*

Published by The Oakwood Press, P.O. Box 13, Usk, Mon., NP15 1YS.
E-mail: oakwood-press@dial.pipex.com
Website: http://ds.dial.pipex.com/oakwood-press

Contents

Birmingham RCW Type '2' No. D5301 in BR green livery is pictured leaving Millerhill with a train of empty HAA hoppers for Bilston Glen in June 1969. *Ken Falconer*

3

Gradient Profile - Glencorse Branch

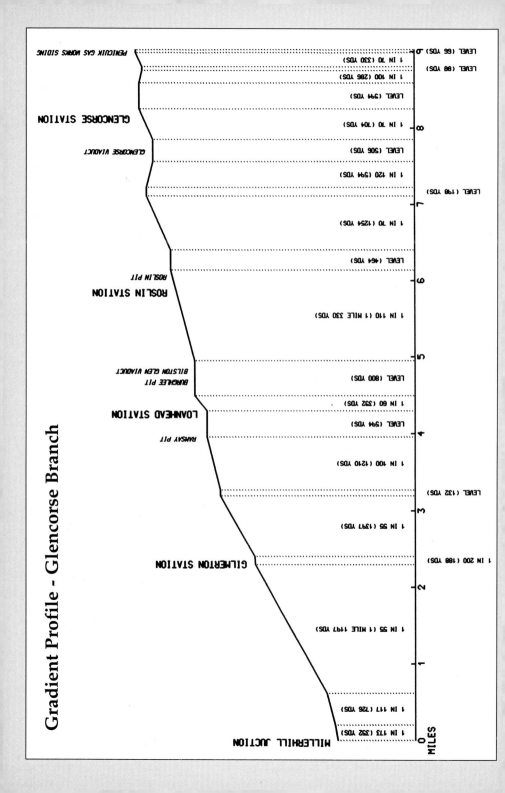

PENICUIK GAS WORKS SIDING

LEVEL (66 YDS)
1 IN 70 (330 YDS)
LEVEL (88 YDS)
1 IN 100 (286 YDS)
LEVEL (394 YDS)
1 IN 70 (704 YDS)
LEVEL (906 YDS)
1 IN 120 (594 YDS)
LEVEL (198 YDS)
1 IN 70 (1254 YDS)
LEVEL (464 YDS)
1 IN 110 (1 MILE 330 YDS)
LEVEL (800 YDS)
1 IN 60 (352 YDS)
LEVEL (594 YDS)
1 IN 100 (1210 YDS)
LEVEL (132 YDS)
1 IN 55 (1397 YDS)
1 IN 200 (188 YDS)
1 IN 55 (1 MILE 1197 YDS)
1 IN 111 (726 YDS)
1 IN 173 (352 YDS)

GLENCORSE STATION

GLENCORSE VIADUCT

ROSLIN PIT

ROSLIN STATION

BILSTON GLEN VIADUCT
BURGHLEE PIT

LOANHEAD STATION

RAMSAY PIT

GILMERTON STATION

MILLERHILL JUCTION

MILES

Acknowledgements

It is very true to say that this book would not have been possible without the co-operation and assistance of a great many people, and the author's thanks are due to all who gave their time so freely. The Edinburgh area is very well served by a large number of archives, and sincere thanks are due to the Staff of the following:

The West Search Room, Scottish Record Office
The National Map Library
The Edinburgh Room of the Central Library, The City of Edinburgh Council
The Records Department of British Coal, Newtongrange
The Scottish Mining Museum, Newtongrange
The Keeper of the Records of Scotland
MacTaggart, Scott & Co. Ltd (Mr P.R. Prenter)
Hunslet Barclay Ltd (Mrs Law)

The assistance provided by Marion Richardson of the Midlothian Council, Department of Local Studies, Loanhead is gratefully acknowledged.

Thanks also to Forbes Alexander, of the Signalling Record Society, who provided the signalling diagrams, and gave permission for Mike Greenlaw to re-draw them for publication. Mike also provided the excellent maps and other artwork.

The author is indebted to Jim Hay for the station drawings.

The 25 inch Ordnance Survey maps are reproduced by permission of the Trustees of the National Library of Scotland, with the sole exception of the map of Gilmerton which was supplied by the Bodleian Library, Oxford.

Thanks are also due to the Committee of Glencorse Golf Club for their assistance and also permission to reproduce the plan on page 50.

The proof reading expertise of Mike Smith was utilised to the full, and considerably eased the transition from thoughts to the written word.

To those individuals who had the foresight to take the photographs, and collect those of earlier times, the author is especially thankful, and for their willingness to allow their inclusion. Any errors in crediting the illustrations is unintentional, as in some cases their origin is unclear. Individuals who helped in particular include Andrew Bethune, Joan Cooney, Bruce Ellis, Andrew Hajducki, David Heathcote, Peter Dickie, Gordon Hewit, Dave King, Bill Lynn, Alistair McArdle, Major R.P. Mason, The Royal Scots, Rae Montgomery, John Rapley, Marshall Shaw, Alan Simpson, the late J.L. Stevenson, Norman Turnbull, Lisa Trotter and Douglas Yuill. Any comments or corrections are welcomed, via the publishers.

If any reader wishes to find out more about the NBR, its constituents and successors, they are recommended to contact Bill Lynn, the Membership Secretary of the North British Railway Study Group, 2, Brecken Court, Saltwell Road South, Low Fell, Gateshead, County Durham, NE9 6EY. From personal experience, I can guarantee a warm welcome.

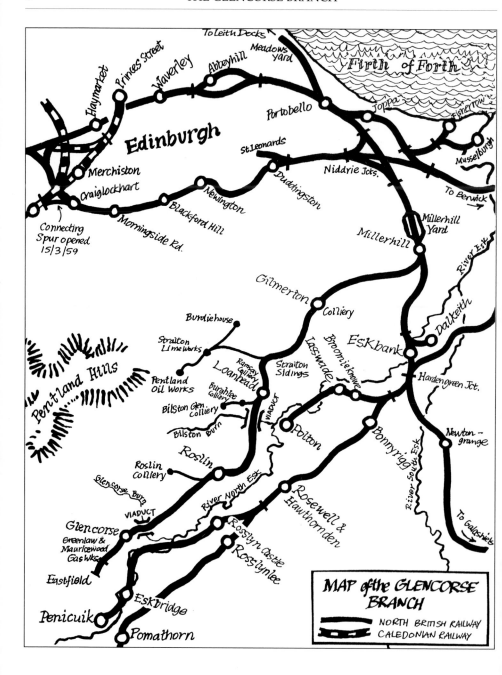

MAP of the GLENCORSE BRANCH

NORTH BRITISH RAILWAY
CALEDONIAN RAILWAY

Introduction

I first 'discovered' the Glencorse branch in the summer of 1963, while exploring the district by means of a recently acquired bicycle and the local Ordnance Survey map. The sight of a very dirty 'B1' running round a rake of 16 ton mineral wagons at Roslin remains as one of my abiding memories to this day.

The Edinburgh, Loanhead and Roslin Railway (ELR) was one of several branches which ran south-west from the northern end of the North British Railway (NBR) Edinburgh-Carlisle main line (the 'Waverley Route'). It remains unique in that it was the last to be completed, the first to lose its passenger service and has outlasted all of them in continuous use, including the Waverley Route itself, by a considerable margin. Indeed, at the time of writing, the rails are still in place, eight years after the passage of the last train.

Although the branch was just over eight miles long, and has never featured prominently in the railway press, I think that it has a story worth telling, and I have attempted to cover, as comprehensively as possible, its history, together with details of the various industries served.

When discussing train services, it should be borne in mind that the use of the terms 'up' and 'down' by the NBR differed from the usual practice. To quote from the NBR General Manager's circular of 1st January, 1868: 'All Trains on the North British system going *southwards* will be designated *Up Trains* and all those proceeding *Northwards* will be called *Down Trains'*. It then follows that branch trains proceeded *Up* to Glencorse, and *Down* to Millerhill.

The subject of Scottish place names can be a source of confusion, and several of the places served by the ELR may require explanation.

Roslin: Before the 15th century, the area was known as 'Roskelyn', then 'Rosslyn' and finally the more modern form 'Roslin'. Either of the latter two spellings were freely used in the last century by the North British Railway in correspondence. To add to the confusion of the prospective passenger, we also have Rosslyn Castle and Rosslynlee stations nearby. This is explained in Chapter Three.

Glencorse: The military barracks here was known as Greenlaw, as is the local farm, but 'Glencross' was used in internal correspondence by the NBR in 1876-1879, before the adoption of the final form 'Glencorse'.

Jeff Hurst
Loanhead,
January 1999

Roslin Castle and Glen.

Roslin Chapel, north front.

Chapter One

History

The area of Midlothian under consideration is as rich in history as it is in minerals, which turned out to be the main reason for the branch's existence. The discovery of large reserves of ironstone nearby in the mid-1860s provided the impetus to improve rail access, while the presence of limestone, shale and coal made the venture even more attractive. However, coal and limestone had been worked for hundreds of years in small quarries scattered along the line of the main geological fault, which runs north-east from Penicuik to the Firth of Forth. There had never been large areas of industrial development in the County of Midlothian, as in West Lothian or Lanarkshire, which had resulted in pits surrounded by green fields and farms. With the progressive decline of the traditional heavy industries, such as coal, successful reclamation schemes have been undertaken in recent years to eradicate the worst of the scars left by these developments, making it difficult to believe, in some cases, that industry had been carried on for as long as it had. Even where it has not been possible to remove waste bings, careful landscaping has lessened their impact on the countryside.

Bounded by the City of Edinburgh to the north, the Pentland Hills to the west, and the River South Esk to the east, the area is surprisingly rural, even today. The site of Gilmerton station, for example, lies within the city boundary, but is still surrounded by farmland, so that a prospective passenger of the 1990s would have almost the same distance to walk from the nearest group of houses as his counterpart of the 1870s. The South Esk and its many tributaries, flowing in a north - easterly direction, has always formed a natural barrier to southbound travellers, forcing them to parallel the Pentland Hills as far as Penicuik, or use the crossing at Lasswade.

Both Loanhead and Roslin were small villages each situated about a mile to the east of the main road from Edinburgh to Penicuik and the south, via Moffat. In the distant past, Loanhead was always referred to as the 'Loanhead of Lasswade', which is taken to mean the place at the head of the 'loan' or lane leading to Lasswade. As with much of this part of Scotland, one of the earliest historical references to the area is a battle, with the defeat of an English army of 30,000 by a Scottish force of 8,000 at Bilston Glen in February 1303. At this period, and for several centuries afterwards, there existed only a few scattered cottages in the vicinity, but by 1528 one Edward Sinclair of Dryden was granted the 'right to win coal upon his property of Dryden and Loanhead'. Some 141 years later, in 1669, Loanhead had expanded sufficiently for the Scottish Parliment to grant a charter to his successor, Sir John Nicholsone, over 'the lands, coals and coal heughs of Loanhead' for the same purpose.

Roslin, or Rosslyn as it was known in older times, has a very different history to that of Loanhead. The name comes from two celtic words, Ross, meaning a rocky promontory, and lynn, a waterfall, both of which are to be found in the nearby North Esk valley. In 1446 it was described as the 'chiefest town in all

Lothian, except Edinburgh and Haddington', due to the many important visitors to the court of King James II, which was held periodically at Rosslyn Castle. In or about 1486, Rosslyn Chapel was completed, which enhanced the status of the village even more. Many visitors have made the journey to see the Chapel and the 'Prentice pillar, and continue to do so to this day.

Coal

While coal had been worked at Loanhead and Penicuik for several centuries, the earliest record of coal working in Midlothian is to be found in a charter given to the monks of Newbattle Abbey between 1210 and 1219. They continued to extract such coal as was easily dug from where it outcropped beside the Whytrig burn, until the Reformation in 1560. Output was very small, and was mainly used for their own domestic purposes. It was also given out at the church door to the poor of the parish, being described in contemporary accounts as 'black stones' or 'sulphurous stone'.

There is evidence that the local landowners were developing coalfields by this time, with Sir John Clerk commencing operations on his Penicuik Estate by 1687, and at Loanhead in 1694. It was at his instigation that improvements to the Ramsey pit in Loanhead were carried out and, by 1728, a tunnel, or 'level', had been driven from a point 40 fathoms down the shaft to the bank of the North Esk, to assist in draining the workings. This played an important part in later years in also draining the pits at Burghlee and Roslin, and remained in use until the closure of the Ramsey pit in 1965, a testimony to the miners who had excavated it entirely by hand.

The Greenlaw Estate, to the north of Penicuik, was sold to Robert Trotter of Bush, whose descendants will figure later in our story, for the high price of £20,348, a figure based on the estimated value of the extensive reserves thought to lie beneath. It fell to his son, John, who had inherited the estate in 1807, to commence the sinking of a colliery in 1842. This proved to be a disaster financially, losing £12,000 alone between 1844 and 1848, as a result of difficultes encountered due to inadequate drainage.

Ironstone

Up until the end of the 18th century, ironstone had been discarded as waste, but the revelation that it could be used in place of imported Swedish ore was welcomed by the iron industry. A further improvement was achieved by the addition of limestone as a flux and the discovery, in the Shotts area of Lanarkshire, of coal, limestone and ironstone led to the establishment of the Shotts Iron Company (SIC) in 1810. A further improvement came in 1832 with the use of hot air in a blast furnace at Shotts, enabling the best use to be made of the ironstone. By the mid-1840s, some 90 furnaces had been established in Lanarkshire, providing an annual turnover of over 5,000,000 tons of pig iron. By the 1850s, the reserves in Lanarkshire were running low and, anxious to secure a supply for the future, the SIC began surveying in other areas. It settled on Midlothian, with test bores being sunk at Loanhead in 1865.

Excellent results were revealed, and by the autumn of 1866, output had risen to over 1,500 tons per month, and to 3,000 tons within a year, all of which had to be transported over a very poor road system, by horse-drawn carts.

Limestone

The properties of limestone as a soil improver and as an ingredient in mortar for building had resulted in it being quarried locally, close to where it was required. With the rise of the iron industry in the 19th century, demand increased far beyond the capacity of local supplies, resulting in the setting up of larger quarries and pits. Midlothian had large deposits of limestone, which outcropped on both sides of the Pentland Hills. In the east, the strata runs in two lines, the first from Carlops to Portobello, with the other following the line of the Midlothian coalfield, from Lamancha to Pathhead, and on to the coast at Aberlady. The limestone found along the Carlops-Portobello line was found to be of high quality, and was named after the Burdiehouse area where it occurred in quantities large enough to be commercially viable. Large kilns were established at an unknown date, certainly before the construction of the branch, beside the quarries immediately east of Burdiehouse village.

Burdiehouse limekilns are a familiar local landmark, albeit dwarfed by the electricity pylons in this June 1995 view.   *Author*

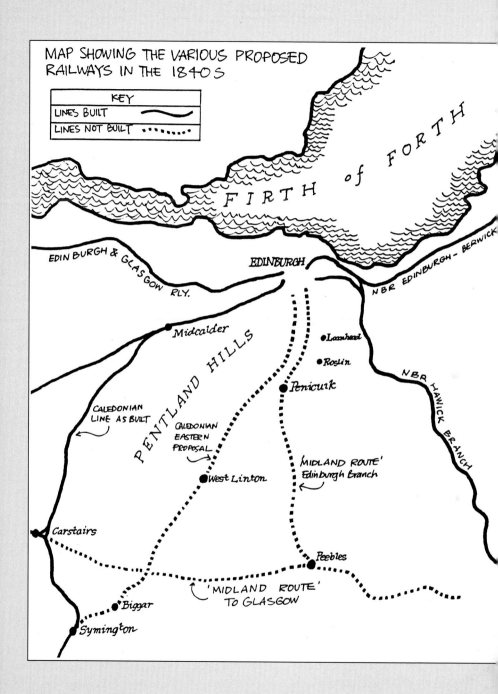

Chapter Two

Earlier Schemes

As the development of the railway system in the area did not start in earnest until the middle 1860s, it could be thought that this part of Midlothian had escaped the attention, thus far, of railway promoters, but at least three schemes had been promoted much earlier in the century, involving eminent railway engineers of the day. No less a person than George Stephenson was involved in the first of these, a line which, if built, would have altered the railway map considerably.

By the 1830s, promoters of the English railway system had been concentrating on the development of the east of the country, which had resulted in a series of lines joining London with the North East, albeit by circuitous routes, when compared with the current system. The promoters' attentions now centred on Scotland, which could be reached with relative ease by the coast, via Berwick, thus avoiding the Southern Uplands, which form a formidable barrier across the border country, dividing the two kingdoms. While this route was by far the logical one, particularly given the low powered locomotives of the day, it did not prevent other routes from being promoted, with little regard to their viability.

The Edinburgh and Dunbar Railway Company was formed in 1836 to promote a line between these two points but, on hearing of a scheme to join Edinburgh and Glasgow with Newcastle by an inland route, it sought the advice of George Stephenson as to its viability as a potential rival. It has to be presumed that the promoters of the former had their sights set eventually on extending their line to Berwick and Newcastle.

In August 1836, George Stephenson presented his report on what he referred to as the 'Midland Line' to the Directors of the Edinburgh and Dunbar Railway Company. The proposed route was roughly parallel to the turnpike road (the modern day A68) from Newcastle to Carter Bar, with a two-mile tunnel through the Cheviot Hills, followed by massive cuttings and embankments with gradients as steep as 1 in 117, a stiff challenge for the locomotives of the period. The line then would have passed through Jedburgh and on to Galashiels, where it would have followed the valley of the Tweed to Peebles. Here the line was to have diverged, the route to Glasgow continuing up the Tweed valley, and the Edinburgh line turning northwards via 'Eddlestone and Pennyciuk' to a terminus near the Tron Church. The section from Leadburn to Edinburgh had gradients of 1 in 66 and 1 in 37, with a section of 1 in 62 for seven miles, prompting Stephenson to observe that 'this could not be worked by locomotive engines, nor does it appear that the gradient can be materially improved'.

Commenting on the whole proposal, he stated that, 'I can scarcely form any conception of the magnitude of such works as I have been describing, never having heard of a continuous succession of such works being attempted.'

Even taking into account that he had an interest in the rival scheme, his conclusions appear to be correct, as nothing more was heard of the 'Midland Line' to Scotland.

Within a year this part of Midlothian saw another party of railway surveyors, this time surveying a route which was intended to approach from the south-west, as part of the Caledonian Railway's West Coast Route to Scotland. As with the various East Coast schemes, a similar situation existed on the west side of the country. This time, however, there was a choice of two suitable routes northwards from Carlisle, via Nithsdale or Annandale, to reach Glasgow, the original objective. The summit of the latter, at Beattock, was again considered to be beyond the power of contemporary locomotives when first put forward, but another leading railway engineer, Joseph Locke, was convinced that this was not an insurmountable problem. Having added Edinburgh to the plan, the route was to split at Symington, in Lanarkshire, to reach the capital, with the choice of passing to the east or west of the Pentland Hills. The easterly route would have passed through Biggar, West Linton and Penicuik to reach a terminus in the Meadows area of Edinburgh, descending Liberton Brae in the process. While this took in more centres of population and sources of potential freight traffic, the severity of the gradients led to it being rejected on cost grounds, despite the saving of several miles. To quote Sir J.H.A. MacDonald the Lord Justice Clerk, in his book *Life Jottings of an Edinburgh Citizen*, published in 1915, 'When the Caledonian line was being surveyed, the proper direction for it was, beyond all doubt, by Penicuik and Biggar valley. But one who had been employed as a young engineer in the laying of it out, assured me that it was not then conceived to be possible to ascend Liberton Hill without the aid of a fixed engine and a rope, and that led, among other causes, to its rejection.' The western route was approved by the Caledonian Railway Board in 1844, but if the decision had come out in favour of the easterly route, it is clear that the railway development of the area would have taken a very different course, and it is interesting to speculate on the possibility of electric-hauled expresses speeding through Penicuik, on their way from Edinburgh to London, via the West Coast route.

The next projected railway to use the North Esk valley, if constructed, would have made the Peebles, Penicuik and the Edinburgh, Loanhead and Roslin railways unnecessary. Engineered by David Stevenson, of Edinburgh, the Peebles Railway proposal of November 1845 would have served Loanhead, Glencorse and Penicuik *en route* to its destination. Separate branches were to connect Lasswade and Roslin with the main line. Leaving the Edinburgh and Dalkeith Railway near to Whitehill farm, south of Newcraighall, it was to proceed by Danderhall and Gilmerton, using almost the same route as the ELR. Immediately after crossing the Edinburgh-Lasswade road, a mile-long branch would have descended initally at 1 in 123, then at 1 in 42 to a terminus at the present road junction at Wadingburn, half a mile from Lasswade village. It is unclear now why the line was not to have been continued down to serve the paper mills in Lasswade, but it may have been that objections had been received from local landowners. The main line, meanwhile, would have carried on towards Loanhead, passing through what is now Inveravon road, where two possible routes were shown, the direct one skirting Bilston Glen to the north, while the alternative was to pass even further north, presumably to avoid possible objections from the owner of the Dryden Estate, as the more southerly route would have cut through the drive to the main house. At the point where this deviation was to re-join the original route, east of the present A701/A703 roundabout, would have been the junction for the ¾ mile Roslin branch. Continuing to keep to the east of the A701, another deviation is shown as, due to the depth of the river North Esk valley opposite Glencorse Barracks, the original route would have cut through part of the property. Therefore an alternative and more northerly course, starting at the present Glencorse Centre and following the eventual course of the ELR was offered. The site of Penicuik station was to have been next to Bridge Street, on the opposite side from that chosen in 1872. Apart from the gradient of 1 in 70 for the first four miles or so, the route was over relatively level ground to Penicuik, but the 1 in 40 gradients required on both sides of the summit at Leadburn would have taxed the locomotives of the day. Perhaps for this reason, and also the perceived lack of potential goods traffic, it also became a 'might have been'.

Having been deprived of a main line to the south, and a line to Peebles, the inhabitants of this part of Midlothian now had to wait 20 years for the next proposal. Despite the fact that the North British Railway had been strengthening its hold on the east and south of Edinburgh, the proposal for a Penicuik branch line promoted in 1864 came from the rival Caledonian Railway (CR). Reaching the town via Morningside and Liberton, it was to be double-tracked throughout, and would have posed a major threat to the NBR, in what was seen as the latter's territory. While the NBR could have been accused of complacency up until now, the threat of the CR incursion galvanised it into action.

The North British Railway (Lasswade, &c. Branches) Act 1865, which was granted the Royal Assent on 19th June, 1865, gave the NBR powers to construct no fewer than six railways (and two public roads) in the area between the St Leonards branch, Edinburgh and the Peebles Railway. The reader is recommended to refer to the map on page 16 for an explanation of the routes of the various lines authorised. Had these been built, they certainly would have put Penicuik and Loanhead on a direct route to the West (via the Edinburgh & Glasgow Railway, which became part of the NBR the same year), thus satisfying the requirements of the Shotts Iron Company (whose blast furnaces were situated in Lanarkshire, as explained in the previous chapter). It is also worth noting that the network of proposed lines would have pre-empted the Suburban line, built some 23 years later. Portobello station would also have been enlarged, with 'sidings, booking offices, sheds, warehouses, watering places, workshops, and other conveniences and erections'. The inclusion of running powers over the Esk Valley Railway is also notable, considering that it had not been built at the time, and that the fifth railway authorised would have diverted traffic away from a large part of the Esk Valley Railway.

The Act specified that all of the works were to be completed within five years, but, in the event, none were started, due to a major upheaval in the NBR Board of Directors in 1866.

The Chairman of the the NBR at this time was Richard Hodgson, of Carham Hall, Coldstream who, for some years, had been pursuing a policy of expansion of the company, particularly if the Caledonian Railway could be prevented

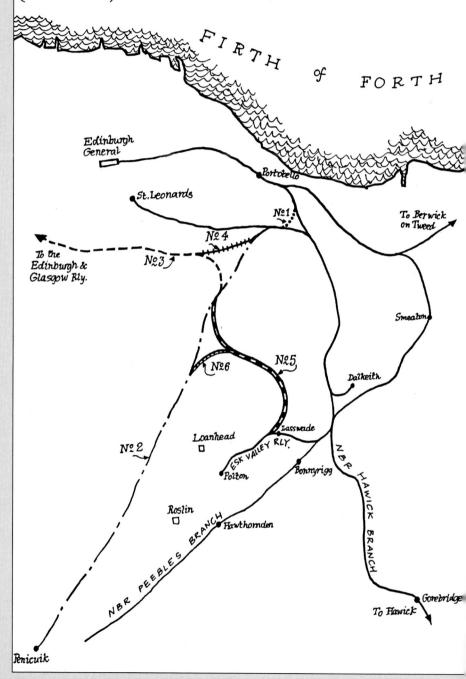

MAP SHOWING THE VARIOUS RAILWAYS PROPOSED BY THE NORTH BRITISH RAILWAY (LASSWADE & BRANCHES) ACT 1865 (28 & 29 VICT.)

from invading North British territory. By November 1866, however, irregularities had been discovered in the company's accounts, with debts amounting to over £1.8 million pounds. As a result, the NBR did not pay an ordinary dividend from the second half of 1866 until the end of 1871. Hodgson, together with 11 of the 15 Directors and the General Manager, was dismissed, and the new Board was in no position to use the Act's powers.

The abandonment left the NBR in a financally embarrassing position with regard to the Shotts Iron Company, which, as explained in Chapter One, had taken leases of local mineral fields. An agreement had been entered into, whereby the NBR had undertaken to 'carry the calcined ironstone of the said Shotts Iron Company from Loanhead to their works in the county of Lanark, at a fixed rate of 3s. 6d. per ton'. Without a railway to carry the traffic, the NBR had been forced to pay for the transport by road to Kevock siding, on the recently opened Esk Valley Railway. This was costing the NBR 1s. per ton, not to mention the loss of potential traffic from other local sources.

At this point, the NBR appears to have adopted its usual practice of encouraging the promotion of local railway companies, offering to work them for a proportion of the receipts and taking them over completely a few years later. In this way, the initial costs and Parliamentary proceedings were avoided, and the companies could be amalgamated later, on terms favourable to the NBR.

CHAP. xlvi.

An Act to authorise the Construction of the Edinburgh, A.D. 1870.
Loanhead, and Roslin Railway. [20th June 1870.]

WHEREAS the making and maintaining of the railway by this
Act authorised would be of local and public advantage:
And whereas the persons herein-after named, with others, desire
to be incorporated into a company for making the said railway:

And whereas plans and sections showing the lines and levels of
the railway, together with books of reference to such plans con-
taining the names of the owners or reputed owners, lessees or reputed
lessees, and of the occupiers of the lands and property required or
which may be taken for the purposes of the undertaking, have been
deposited for public inspection in the office of the principal sheriff
clerk of the county of Edinburgh, and those plans, sections, and
books of reference are in this Act referred to as the deposited plans,
sections, and books of reference:

And whereas the objects aforesaid cannot be effected without the
authority of Parliament:

May it therefore please Your Majesty that it may be enacted;
and be it enacted by the Queen's most Excellent Majesty, by and
with the advice and consent of the Lords Spiritual and Temporal,
and of the Commons, in this present Parliament assembled, and
by the authority of the same, as follows:

1. This Act may be cited for all purposes as " The Edinburgh, Short title.
Loanhead, and Roslin Railway Act, 1870."

2. "The Companies Clauses Consolidation (Scotland) Act, 1845," Provisions
Parts I. and III. of "The Companies Clauses Act, 1863," (relating of general
respectively to the cancellation and surrender of shares, and to named incor-
debenture stock,) "The Companies Clauses Act, 1869," "The porated.
Lands Clauses Consolidation (Scotland) Act, 1845," "The Lands
Clauses Consolidation Acts Amendment Act, 1860," "The Railways
Clauses Consolidation (Scotland) Act, 1845," and Parts I. and III.
of "The Railways Clauses Act, 1863," (relating respectively to

[*Local.-46.*] A 1

Chapter Three

The Edinburgh, Loanhead & Roslin Railway

The 'Edinburgh, Loanhead & Roslin Railway Act 1870 received the Royal Assent on 20th June,1870, and empowered the company to construct,

A railway (on the deposited plans and sections called Railway No. 1) six miles, one furlong and 3.2 chains in length, commencing by a junction with the North British Railway, in the parish of Newton, and County of Edinburgh, near the Millerhill station, and terminating in the parish of Lasswade, and County of Edinburgh, at a point in a field called Longpark, twelve yards or thereby from the northern fence of the road from Roslin to Auchindinny, and sixty yards or thereby from the fence forming the south-western boundary of the grounds of Roslin Free Church manse.

The original intention had been to continue the line to Penicuik but, for the reasons explained to the shareholders at the first General Meeting, the proposal had been abbreviated to terminate at Roslin. At this meeting, held at Messrs Millar, Allardice & Robson, W.S., 8 Bank St, Edinburgh, on 14th September, 1870 at '12 o'clock forenoon', only two of the six shareholders who attended were appointed Directors, along with W. White Millar, one of the partners, who acted as Secretary. The minutes state,

The Directors have to report that the line, as originally laid out, commenced by a junction with the North British Railway at Millerhill, and terminated at a point in a field close to a bridge crossing the Esk to the south of the village of Penicuik. After the Parliamentary notice had been given for the line, a second Notice appeared of a line promoted by another company, commencing by a junction with the Peebles Railway near to the Hawthornden station and terminating at the same point as the ELR. It was found from the plans that, after passing Dalmore Mill, the routes were the same.

It is difficult to see how the Shotts Iron Company's traffic from Mauricewood would have been accommodated if the line were to have passed Dalmore, on its way to Penicuik, due to the steep-sided river valley at this point. The ELR's offer of a joint venture was declined and, rather than become embroiled in expensive litigation, the line was cut back to Roslin, with powers to extend later. This decision resulted in the Bill passing through Parliament unopposed, but led to all manner of problems in the future, when the powers were taken up.

The first Directors of the company were:

Sir Simon Lockhart (Bt) of Lee (who had agreed to become a Director on the death of his brother, Sir Norman, who is named in the Act)
Hector Fredrick McLean, Esq. W.S. (Edinburgh)
Hezekiah Merricks, Jnr. (Eskhill)
Lt Col Robert Archibald Trotter of Bush
John Weir Esq., 3 Minto Street, Edinburgh
The post of Secretary was taken by William White Millar, Edinburgh.
The Directors retained their office only until this meeting, but were eligible for re-election.

The inclusion of Hezikiah Merricks in the list of Directors is interesting, as the gunpowder works in Roslin Glen was run by the Merricks family, but no mention is made of encouraging this traffic to the ELR, presumably due to the fact that the Penicuik Railway, under construction at this period, would have been better placed geographically to accommodate it.

Details of traffic expected to use the line were given to the meeting, confidence being expressed that Gilmerton, Loanhead and Dryden coal would be opened up, as would the 'large passenger traffic of the district'. The Shotts Iron Co. had assured the Directors that 50,000 to 60,000 tons of ironstone at least could be forwarded annually, and the Glasgow Iron Co. already had commenced sinking a pit on land leased at Gilmerton. Provision would also be made for the Straiton and Burdiehouse traffic, by constructing a short branch to each of these places. The 'cordial' support of the local landowners was also expected although, as events were to show, this expectation did not materialise fully.

The Directors noted that they had appointed one of the eminent railway engineers of the day, Thomas Bouch, to build the line, and that, in turn, he had recommended his usual contractor, John Waddell, of Bathgate.

Bouch's career was at its zenith by 1870, and his services were in great demand throughout the east of Scotland, with many lines to his credit. These included the St Andrews, Peebles and Esk Valley railways, as well as the street tramways of Edinburgh, Glasgow and Dundee. He was also the Engineer of the South Durham & Lancashire Union Railway, over the Pennines from Barnard Castle to Tebay, where his Deepdale and Belah viaducts stood for over 100 years. Unfortunately, the same could not be said of his best known work, the Tay Bridge, building of which was also started in 1871, but as is well known, fell during a gale in 1879, taking a passenger train with it. There were no such problems with the structures on the ELR, with one exception, as will be recounted in a later chapter. As he could not possibly supervise all of the many contracts with which his office was dealing at this time, he relied on a team of assistants, one of whom, George Trimble, was delegated to deal with the ELR contract.

John Waddell was also a well known figure at this period, having secured many of Bouch's contracts, (he even owned and ran an entire railway company in South Wales, the Llanelly & Mynydd Mawr, whose history is available from The Oakwood Press (OL84)).

The NBR had agreed to work the line for a period of 30 years from the date of opening, for 45 per cent of the gross revenue, while the ELR was also to receive 1s. per ton of limestone sent by the Shotts Iron Co. Significantly, the NBR was also given powers to purchase the line within five years of opening.

Work commenced at Glimerton in November 1871 and proceeded very slowly, due to exceptionally wet weather, which was to dog the contractor intermittently whilst construction proceeded. The rainfall figures published by the Edinburgh Water Trust for the period from January-June 1872 show that 26¾ inches of rain fell in the district, twice the amount that was to fall in 1873.

An entry in the company cash book dated 29th February, 1872 indicates that the Directors had found it necessary to employ a police constable, at £2 2s. 0d. per fortnight. This was common practice, where no local police presence existed. He received a uniform allowance of £3 3s. 0d. and 2s. 'boot money', which had to last six months.

In May 1872 an offer was received from the steelmakers Redpath, Brown for the supply of a quantity of rails, but this was declined, as the Committee thought that the NBR might be a cheaper source. This appears to have been the case, as a mile of rails was purchased from them the following month. From then on the NBR supplied all of the trackwork, while naturally charging the ELR for carriage.

The following July meeting formally approved the working agreement with the NBR, and delegated Sir James Falshaw and the Secretary to attend a meeting to discuss the naming of local stations. Although there would be no prospect of the line opening for some considerable time, the prospect of confusion over the names of the stations on the various local lines now in progress had prompted the Penicuik Railway to call the meeting with the Peebles Railway and the ELR for 1st September, 1872. The Peebles company announced that it would not attend, as 'they did not see the need for it'. Possibly, as its line was first in the area, it adopted the attitude that it was the other companies' responsibility to name their stations so as to avoid confusion. This was the start of a long running saga, as we shall see.

A letter received from the NBR, discussed at the August meeting, asked the Board to proceed with the extension to Glencorse, and Waddell was encouraged to employ extra workers in order to speed up progress. This was the start of a NBR campaign to have the extension built, to enable the latter to fulfill the agreement with the SIC, as output from Mauricewood pit was still travelling by road.

The fifth half-yearly General Meeting, held on 9th October, 1872, is the first to include a Engineer's Report, which is worth repeating:

Earthwork:
About 68,000 cubic yards have been deposited in embankment and into spoil.
Rock:
Nearly 20,000 cubic yards have been deposited in embankment, and what is suitable has been prepared for ballast.
Masonry:
The Turnpike Road Bridges at 59 chains, 63 chains and at 1 mile 26 chains are built up to impost height, and are ready for the girders. The occupation bridge at 1 mile 26 chains, under railway, is also ready for the girders, and the approaches are finished. The occupation bridge at 2 miles 32 chains is finished, except the parapet, coping and iron railing. The Turnpike Road Bridge at 3 miles 69 chains, over the railway, is in progress, and nearly to the required height. The Street bridges at Loanhead are in progress, and a portion of the girders in place, and the public traffic is on both roads.These bridges will be completed in about three weeks.
Bilston Glen Viaduct:
The foundations of the first pier have been put in, and brickwork commenced.
Fencing:
Post and rail fencing for 10,000 yards are in place.
Permanent Way:
1,500 yards of rails have been laid down and partly ballasted. About 110 yards are bottom ballasted, and ready for the permanent way.
Materials on ground:
8,759 sleepers and 40 tons of chairs are provided.

I have the honour to be, Gentlemen, your most obedient Servant,

Thomas Bouch

The Directors' report outlined the lack of progress on the line between Millerhill and Loanhead, which they had hoped would have been open by the time of the meeting, at least for mineral traffic. The 'unprecedented wet weather during the spring and summer months' was given as the cause. On the Roslin section, the contractor had recently been given possession of the land, with one exception, and work had started on Bilston viaduct. A new estimated opening date of June 1873 was offered, provided that the weather remained favourable over the winter.

The Directors were under ever increasing pressure over the Glencorse extension, and the NBR General Manager, Samuel Mason, had written to the Board on 1st November, 1872, indicating that it could not undertake the extension under the terms of the present agreement, but that if the ELR did not agree to new terms (details of which are not included in the minutes), the NBR would take over the extension powers, and relieve the ELR of all expenses and liability.

The Secretary, who appears to have been unpaid since his appointment in October 1871, had his salary fixed at £72 per annum at a Board meeting on 19th December, 1872. However, he had to wait until 31st January, 1873 before receiving the £96 due to him. The third call of £2 per share was also made, along with the instruction that a further supply of rails be obtained at £11 10s. 0d. 'or cheaper'.

The weather had further delayed construction during the period December 1871 to January 1872, to the effect that only two-thirds of the 180,000 cubic yards of cutting required had been excavated by the end of February 1873. The two bridges in the centre of Loanhead were finished, and several others required only the girders to complete them. The three tallest piers of Bilston viaduct were only 40 ft short of their required height, and the foundations of the remaining two had been started. Considering that the viaduct was to rise 150 feet above the Bilston Burn, and that the area was covered in thick woodland, the problems in reaching the site can be imagined.

When the route through Loanhead had been decided, the surveyors had taken the line through the very centre which, while benefiting potential travellers, had meant building the line across the Bowling Club property. Bowling was, and indeed still is, a very popular local pastime, and the club received £25 compensation for the loss of its ground. This appears to be a very modest amount, when it could be seen that landowners were receiving a similar sum per acre for their land taken up by the railway.

At a special meeting held immediately after the normal Board meeting on 5th February, 1872, approval was given to the Bill to extend the line to Glencorse and Mauricewood, to be submitted to Parliament without delay. If the Directors had thought that the decision over the Extension Bill would keep the NBR happy, their thoughts were to be dashed within a few weeks, when the Board received a letter which indicated that the NBR expected the major part of the cost of the new junction at Millerhill to be met by the ELR. The plans for the junction had been discussed at the Board meeting at the end of February, along with the suggestion that Loanhead should be provided with a 'double passing place'. In view of the projected level of traffic from the extension line, this appears to have been a sensible idea. George Trimble had presented the junction plans and it appears that the Directors had assumed that they would not be expected to make a substantial financial contribution, nor were they prepared to pay towards all of the land required. The Board decided to offer a maximum of £3,000 to be spent on the junction, and so informed the NBR General Manager by letter on 13th March, 1872. The opposite view was, of course, held by the NBR, and the dispute carried on until June before an agreement was reached.

On a brighter note the contract for the building of the stations was let on 28th April, 1872 to Messrs Robertson, who had submitted the lowest tender of £1,047. Agreement was reached also with Colonel Trotter, who was one of the shareholders, over two of his tenants' cottages, which had been demolished to make way for the railway. A payment of £200 was made, rather than undertake the rebuilding on another site. At a meeting with the Penicuik Railway Board on 16th May, 1872, the station name issue was finally decided, with 'Rosslyn Castle' station on the Penicuik Railway and 'Roslin' on the ELR.

It was now becoming clear to the Board that they must reach an agreement over the junction with the NBR, otherwise the opening of the line would be further delayed. Accordingly, the NBR Engineer, James Bell, was asked to prepare an estimate on 28th May, 1872. One week later the estimate was with the Secretary, giving the costs as follows:

NBR share - £1648 10s. 0d.
ELR share - £3331 15s. 0d.

In contrast to the original Bill, that for the Glencorse Extension had an easy passage through Parliament, gaining the Royal Assent on 5th August, 1872, even though the original line was nowhere near completion. Capital was fixed at £36,000, and two railways were authorised:

No. 1 - 2 miles, 3 furlongs, 113 yards or thereabouts in length, commencing by a junction with the authorised Edinburgh, Loanhead, and Roslin Railway, and terminating in the parish of Glencorse, otherwise Glencross, all in the County of Edinburgh.
No. 2 - 5 furlongs and 67 yards or thereabouts in length, commencing in the parish of Glencorse, otherwise Glencross, at the point hereinbefore described as the termination of Railway No. 1, and terminating in the parish of Penicuik, all in the County of Edinburgh.

At last, the ELR would be able to fulfil its original remit, and accommodate the Shotts Iron Company's traffic from Mauricewood. However, the more immediate task was to open the line as far as Loanhead, and, although the Board had reached an agreement with the NBR over Millerhill Junction on 16th August 1872, Waddell made it clear that he was not satisfied with the arrangement. The cost of land and earthworks had been excluded from the NBR estimate, and he notified the Board on 28th August that he would not undertake the earthworks without extra payment. The Board reacted to this by instructing the Secretary to inform Waddell that the earthworks should be put in hand immediately, using another contractor if necessary, wholly at Waddell's expense. This appears to have had the desired effect, as the matter disappears from the Minute Book.

There is no indication in the next Directors' report, prepared for the seventh half-yearly meeting on 30th September, 1873, of the problem over the Junction earthworks; only that agreement had been reached with the NBR 'to form the necessary Sidings and construct the Junction at Millerhill, as well as to erect the necessary Signals.'

Three of the Directors, including John Weir and Sir James Falshaw, had made a personal inspection of the work in progress on the Monday previous to the date of the meeting, from the viaduct to Millerhill, and could report from personal experience 'that the line was perfectly clear all that distance, with the track laid and ballasting in progress'. Both Gilmerton and Loanhead stations and sidings, it was predicted, would be finished by the middle of the month, and it was hoped to start mineral traffic early in November 1873.

This report is the first to indicate that the Loanhead mineral traffic should be given priority over the opening of the line to passengers, which would have to wait until the Bilston viaduct to Roslin section of the branch was ready. Some progress was reported on this section, with the earthwork south of the viaduct complete up to the site of Roslin station, and the piers of the viaduct ready to accept the girders.

Another difficulty had been overcome the previous day, when the site for Roslin station had been bought from the Lasswade School Board. The matter of finding a central site for the station in Roslin had been causing some concern, as the most suitable one was already occupied by the local school, and the Board eventually followed Bouch's advice and offered the School Board the 'very ample sum' of £400 for the building.

A vote of thanks to the Directors was proposed by a Mr Corner, of Whitby, who thought that the prospects of the line were exceptionally good and, as Roslin was one of the favourite resorts of tourists visiting Edinburgh, he thought that the station there 'should possess something of an ornamental character'.

The fact that the branch was nearing completion had been circulated to the various departments of the NBR which would be involved with the day to day running. Thomas Wheatley, the locomotive superintendent, was informed by the General Manager on 2nd October, 1873. The Locomotive Department of the NBR was usually the last to hear of matters concerning it, and this is borne out by Mr Wheatley's reply, sent the next day: 'I suppose it will be brought by one engine, same as other branches. It will require to be provided with shed accommodation and a sufficient supply of good water, and please let me know whether it will require a tank or tender engine to work it.' His reference to the water supply is significant, as will become clear later. He must have assumed also that the NBR would be handling the traffic from the opening date, which was not the case.

On 9th October the NBR general superintendent, James McLaren, requested details of the branch stations and respective mileages, which were given as follows:

Station	Miles	Chains
Millerhill	0	0
Gilmerton	2	21
Shotts Sidings (Ramsey Pit)	3	75
Loanhead Station	4	16
Shotts Sidings (Burghlee Pit)	4	50
Roslin Station	5	69

By 28th October Wheatley, not having had a reply to his enquiry, sent a reminder, which also appears to have been ignored. Two days later the NBR announced, in its Circular No. M223, the 'Opening of the New Loanhead and Rosslyn Branch Junction', to be opened at 12 o'clock noon on Thursday 6th November, 1873. A detailed description of the new signalling arrangements followed, plus the relevant engine whistle codes.

The NBR made it clear to the ELR that it had no intention of allowing its locomotives to run on the branch just yet, preferring to leave wagons at Millerhill for Waddell to deal with. To avoid unecessary shunting at the junction, NBR 'break van' No. 32 was sent to Millerhill for use by the contractor. Until facilities were completed at Ramsey Colliery, weighing of wagons would be carried out at Niddrie, under instructions from the NBR goods manager, Mr Rutherford, who also requested a starting date for the Shotts Iron Co's traffic.

As the line was to carry the SIC traffic only meantime, inspection by the Board of Trade (BoT) was not required until passenger services started. The serving army officers who carried out these inspections were drawn from the Railway Operating Division of the Royal Engineers, and had a great deal of experience in the building and operation of railways. They also carried out accident investigations, and were well known for their professionalism and thoroughness.

The alterations at the new junction at Millerhill were deemed ready for inspection by the last week of October 1873, and the BoT instructed Captain Tyler on 30th October to carry out an inspection as soon as possible. With the nationwide expansion of the railway system at this time, he was unable to visit the junction until late in November, and he submitted his report on 1st December, 1873. He was impressed by the 'excellent' signal cabin and the fact that the points and signals were interlocked with each other, as this practice, which seems logical today, had not been universally adopted by the railway companies of the day. He did stipulate that the facing points should be fitted with locking bars (to prevent them being operated as a train passed over them) and a second tie bar also be added to the points on the branch. He also noted that the proposed passenger arrangements would remain for inspection prior to the ELR being opened for passenger traffic.

To obtain an account of the opening day, Thursday 6th November, 1873, we have to rely on the report published in the next day's *Scotsman* newspaper which saw fit to include the announcement next to the proceedings of the Bankruptcy Court! The Minute Book makes no mention of the event; probably the Directors were only too pleased to see the line partly open, even if only for mineral traffic.

Early in the day, a locomotive and a single carriage conveyed the Directors, contractor and Engineer on a tour of inspection, proceeding slowly along the line to Gilmerton, where 'a minute inspection of the station arrangements was made'. Having continued on to Loanhead, the trackwork was also inspected, which confirms that the station buildings were not finished at this point, and did not merit inclusion. The assembled company then boarded the train for the short journey to the limit of the rails, at the north end of the viaduct. From here the party continued on foot to Roslin, where 'various points of detail were entered into for the better convenience of an anticipated large passenger traffic'. As the buildings had not been started, and no track laid, the inspection could not have taken very long to complete. The day was rounded off with a dinner in the Roslin Hotel, with Mr Wood, the local manager of the Shotts Iron Co. as their guest, at a total cost of £3 16s. 6d.

With the possibility of the line opening sometime in 1874, the NBR thought it a good idea to discover the state of the works on the branch for itself, and instructed the Area Engineer, James Bell, to inspect the line on its behalf. Accordingly, he spent Christmas Day, 1873 walking the line as far as Loanhead. His handwritten report, which is reproduced in full as Appendix Three, gives an insight into the construction of a typical branch line of the period.

It was one thing to have part of the line open for mineral traffic, but the race was now on to have the entire line open to Roslin for all traffic. Everything from clocks for the stations to a locomotive turntable had to be ordered and installed, before the line could be ready for inspection by the Board of Trade.

Estimates were received in February 1874 from Messrs Cowans, Sheldon of Carlisle for a 25 ft diameter turntable, to be installed on the engine shed road at Roslin, at a cost of £375. Although passenger trains were to be worked by tank locomotives, it was normal NBR practice at that time to turn them at branch termini, therefore only a small turntable was necessary. Rothbury, in Northumberland, at the terminus of the branch from Scotsgap, was another example of this practice. A water tank, to be installed at Roslin for locomotive purposes, and cranes for the various goods yards were ordered from James Tod & Son of Leith. The cranes were of three different capacities, no doubt reflecting the Board's estimation of local traffic:

Station	Capacity	Cost
Gilmerton	3 tons	£33 15s. 0d.
Loanhead	5 tons	£60
Roslin	1.5 tons	£28 10s. 0d.

Shareholders attending the half-yearly meeting on 31st March, 1874 were given the good news that 7,637 tons of minerals had been carried since the opening date to 31st January, 1874, earning £1,097 11s. 1d. The working expenses incurred by the NBR had to be deducted from this amount, but the Directors considered that the figures were encouraging, and recommended that the payment of a dividend should wait until the the next half-year. The Engineer's report was equally encouraging, with all bridges complete, the viaduct only requiring the addition of minor bracing, and the track ballasted up to the viaduct. Loanhead and Gilmerton stations had been finished, and Roslin

The North British Railway Company.

——o——

No. 223.

Edinburgh, 30th October 1873.

Notice to Enginemen, Guards, Telegraph Officers, and others.

Opening of the New Loanhead and Rosslyn Branch Junction.

The above New Junction, which will be called "Millerhill. Junction," will be opened at 12 o'clock noon on THURSDAY, 6TH NOVEMBER 1873, and at the same time the undermentioned New Semaphore Signals, connected with the New Millerhill Junction, will be brought into use:—

1. An Up Distant Signal, placed about 800 yards out from the Junction.

2. A two-armed Up Home Signal, placed near the Junction Points: the Higher Arm regulates Main Line Trains, and the Lower Arm regulates Trains going to the Branch.

3. A two-armed Siding Signal, placed on the left hand side of the Brick Works Siding: the Higher Arm regulates Trains leaving the Brick Works Siding, and the Lower Arm regulates Trains leaving the Up Shunting Siding.

4. A Signal for the regulation of Trains entering the Brick Work Siding and Up Shunting Siding, placed near the points connecting the Sidings with Up Main Line.

5. An Advance Starting Signal, placed on the side of the Up Line at a point about 350 yards south of the Junction.

6. A Main Line Down Distant Signal, placed about 800 yards out from the Junction.

7. A Main Line Down Home Signal, being the Highest Arm on the three-armed post placed about 80 yards south of the New Cabin: the Centre Arm regulates Trains proceeding from the Down Shunting Siding to Main Line, and the Lowest Arm regulates Trains proceeding from Down Shunting Siding to Branch Dock Siding.

8. A Down Starting Signal, placed a short distance beyond the north end of Down Platform.

9. A Branch Down Distant Signal, placed near the first over-bridge.

10. A Branch Down Home Signal, placed on the slope at the end of the cutting.

11. A Branch Up Starting Signal, placed near the end of the double line.

12. A two-armed post stands on the side of the Up Line near the Cabin: the Higher Arm regulates Trains proceeding from the Branch to Main Line, and the Lower Arm regulates Trains entering the Dock Siding from the Branch.

* 13. A two-armed post stands between the Dock Siding and Main Line: the Higher Arm regulates Trains proceeding from Dock Siding to Branch Up Line, and the Lower Arm regulates Trains proceeding from same Siding to Down Shunting Siding.

* 14. A Signal for the regulation of Trains leaving the Branch Siding, placed near the catch points of that Siding.

* NOTE.—Nos. 13 and 14.—These Signals are not yet ready, and will be brought into use on a subsequent date, as to which further notice will be given.

All the above New Signals must be worked in strict accordance with the General Regulations of the Company applicable to Junction Signals.

Notice to Enginemen, Guards, Telegraph Officers, and others,
North British Railway, 30th October, 1873.

I. Drivers getting a Clear Home Signal must not assume that the Line is clear to the next Station in advance, but be prepared to stop at the Advance Starting Signal if at "Danger."

II. No Train or Engine must pass an Advance Starting Signal till it is lowered to "All Right."

III. One object of the Advance Starting Signals being to prevent the unnecessary stoppage of Trains, Drivers are required, in all cases where they are allowed to pass the Home Signal while the advance Starting Signal is at "Danger," to run over the intervening space at such slow speed as will afford opportunity for having the Advance Starting Signal lowered, so as to save the necessity for the Drivers bringing their Trains to a dead stand.

IV. A Telegraph Signalman allowing a Train or Engine to proceed up to the Advance Starting Signal must be careful to satisfy himself that such Train or Engine is quite clear of the fouling points before taking on another Train or Engine.

V. Telegraph Signalmen must be equally careful to put the Advance Starting Signals to "Danger" immediately after the passing of every Train or Engine.

STEAM WHISTLES.

Main Line,- - - - - - - -	ONE WHISTLE.
Main Line to Branch, or *vice versa*,- - - - -	TWO WHISTLES.
Branch to Dock Siding, or *vice versa*, - - - -	THREE ,,
To Brickworks Siding, or *vice versa*, - - - -	FOUR ,,
To Up Shunting Siding, or *vice versa*, - - - -	FIVE ,,
Main Line to Down Shunting Siding, or *vice versa*, - -	SIX ,,
Dock Siding to Down Shunting Siding, or *vice versa*, - -	SEVEN ,,
To Branch Siding, or *vice versa*, - - - - -	EIGHT ,,

SAM. L. MASON, General Manager.

Acknowledgment to be signed, cut off, and returned to General Superintendent's Office by first Train.

Date,———————————————1873.

I hereby acknowledge to have received Copies of Circular (M—No. **223**), dated 30th October 1873, in reference to "Opening of the New Loanhead and Rosslyn Branch Junction," to which I shall attend.

Signature,———————————————

Occupation,———————————————

Station,———————————————

Notice to Enginemen, Guards, Telegraph Officers, and others,
North British Railway, 30th October, 1873.

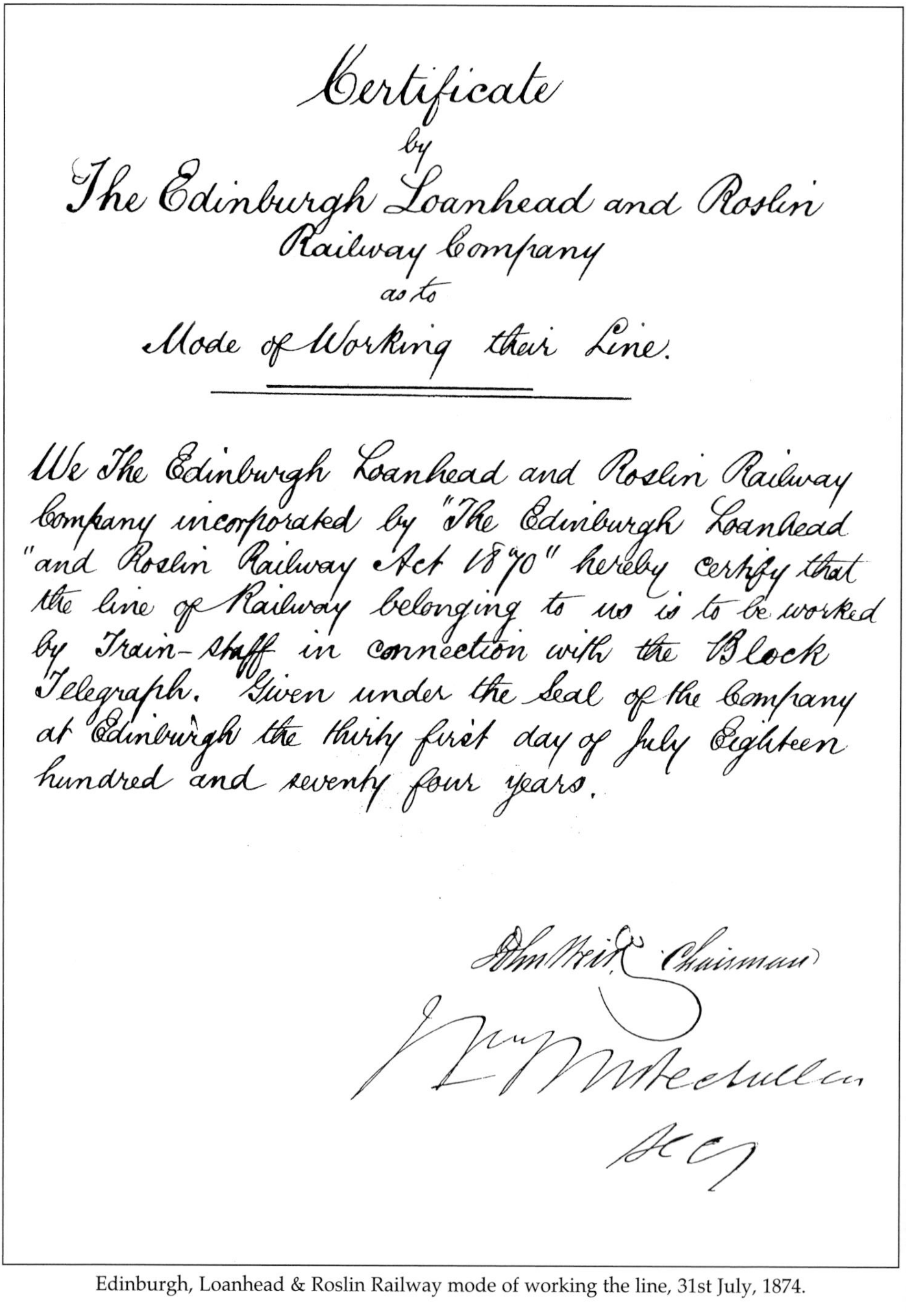

Certificate
by
The Edinburgh Loanhead and Roslin
Railway Company
as to
Mode of Working their Line.

We The Edinburgh Loanhead and Roslin Railway
Company incorporated by "The Edinburgh Loanhead
"and Roslin Railway Act 1870" hereby certify that
the line of Railway belonging to us is to be worked
by Train-staff in connection with the Block
Telegraph. Given under the Seal of the Company
at Edinburgh the thirty first day of July Eighteen
hundred and seventy four years.

John Weir Chairman

Wm Mitchell

Secy

Edinburgh, Loanhead & Roslin Railway mode of working the line, 31st July, 1874.

was expected to be ready by the end of May. As the line was so near to completion, the Board saw no advantage in calling in the Board of Trade Inspector twice, and therefore advised the shareholders that the entire line would open throughout, hopefully by the end of May. The shareholders were also asked, almost as an afterthought, to authorise the Directors to borrow a maximum of £16,000, as the original capital had been insufficient to cover the expenditure to date.

In May the subject of a locomotive water supply at Roslin was raised again, as nothing suitable had been found. Messrs Weir and Rose were authorised to negotiate with the Earl of Rosslyn and the local authorities to solve the problem.

The contractor agreed to maintain the line for a six month period, beginning 25th June, after which the NBR would take over responsibility. At last the Board felt that the line was ready for inspection, and on 2nd July duly submitted the necessary forms, indicating that the ELR would be ready for inspection 'at any time during the ten days next following the 7th day of July'. Only two days later, the Secretary wrote again to the BoT, asking for an early date of inspection 'in order to catch the Tourist Summer Traffic to Roslin'.

Colonel Rich was appointed by a BoT minute dated 6th July, 1874, which informed him that the undertaking as to the method of working the line would be handed to him during the inspection, which was arranged for 22nd July. The BoT were very strict over the methods used to work new railways, due to past experience with railway companies who would avoid any expense which they thought unnecessary. The 'undertaking' was dated 20th July, 1874, and indicated that the line would be worked by the Train Staff.

In his report, Col Rich concurs with the earlier NBR report as regards the suitability of the track, but he was not impressed with the pointwork, which he described as 'excessively clumsy, being about ½ in. to ¾ in. thick at the point, the stock rail being bent to house the blade. This form of point is very bad and should be abandoned by the North British Railway Company. The Company have agreed to chip, file and adjust the whole of the defective points, and to take out one set of facing points at Loanhead at once.' He directed also that a set of facing points serving a quarry at Edgefield, which had been opened by Waddell to provide stone for the structures on the line, be removed until such time as locking bars had been provided. While this was a setback, the Board would have been pleased to note that Col Rich described the bridges and earthworks as 'well carried out, the iron girders are suffciently strong by calculation and gave moderate deflections when loaded'. Having been assured that the various items would be attended to within 10 days, his recommendation was that the line could be opened after this period, provided that the company also submitted a modified statement as to the method of working the line.

By their letter dated 22nd July, the BoT officially forwarded the Inspector's report to the ELR, and stated that a new undertaking would be required, this time giving the method of working by Train Staff and the Block Telegraph. This replacement undertaking was sent on 31st July, and the BoT finally gave their sanction to open the line by their letter reference R5486, dated 1st August, 1874.

At the monthly Board meeting held on the 30th July, the euphoria of almost having a working railway at last must have been dampened slightly by the news that the men employed by the Shotts Iron Co. had struck work, thus temporarily depriving the company of the very traffic which the line had been built to carry. The strike, however, did not last long.

Waddell's offer for the extension line was put on the table, but after some discussion, which included the proposal that the line should be built as far as Milton Cottages meantime, it was resolved to wait until an agreement had been signed with the NBR and arrangements made with the SIC as to the latter's contribution to the construction costs. Waddell's guarantee period was now to start from 23rd July, the NBR paying him working expenses up to this date.

It would appear that the NBR had been stung by the BoT Inspector's remarks about the pointwork, as a letter was received from James Bell on 7th August, agreeing to their replacement, but asserting that 'the same type are used all over the NBR' In fact, they were not replaced until the end of the month, with facing point locks from Saxby and Farmer being fitted at the same time. These alterations presumably satisfied Col Rich on his return visit, the date of which unfortunately is not recorded.

The Board were now open to 'suggestions' from the NBR on all matters concerning the running of the line, and the first of these was a request for a platform 'for the collection of tickets' to be sited near Roslin station. The logic behind this is not clear, as the staff were employed by the NBR, not the ELR, therefore there would have been no advantage in having a separate platform. The Board, to their credit, showed that they were not to be intimidated by the larger company, and replied that if the NBR wanted a platform 'they must erect it themselves'. As there is no record of the existence of a platform, it must be assumed that the NBR had second thoughts.

The proposal from the NBR Traffic Committee that a house be provided for the station master at Loanhead was agreed, the offer of £457 from Robertson being accepted, while that of the proprietor of the Loanhead gasworks, Mr Kay, to provide gas lighting at the station was declined on cost grounds. The gasworks was one of the local businesses which had benefited from the lower cost of coal deliveries, being sited in the nearby High Street. A booking clerk was also added to the NBR staff at Loanhead, at £30 per year.

The SIC had informed the Board that the source of the water supply at Roslin was not to be relied on, and that an offer of a 21 year agreement at £35 per year from the Roslin Paper Association had been received. This was considered to be high, but further negotiations were authorised. The SIC had also offered to pay £5,000 towards the Glencorse extension, provided that it was built within the next 18 months, which prompted the Board to canvass both the NBR and the Glasgow Iron Co. for contributions.

George Wieland, the NBR Secretary, had written to the Board indicating that passengers were confused by the names of stations in the area, resulting in them often ending up in the wrong place. With the opening of the branch, there were now three routes available from Edinburgh, Roslin on the ELR, Rosslyn Castle on the Penicuik Railway, and Pomathorn on the Peebles Railway, (which had been called Penicuik until the Penicuik Railway itself opened in 1872). The Directors , while agreeing that the situation could be confusing, did not see how they could help, as their line was the only one to serve Roslin directly.

It was estimated from the traffic returns that a 3 per cent dividend might be paid, but an announcement would wait until the next shareholders' meeting, on 30th September, 1874.

Bouch was instructed to prepare plans for the extension, in sections, in case it was not taken to the full distance. It is difficult to see the reasoning behind this decision as the extension was already divided in two parts, Roslin-Glencorse and Glencorse-Penicuik. Perhaps the length of time taken to build the first part of the line, and the bank overdraft had made the Board overcautious.

At the shareholders' meeting, it was noted that the Board could now count the Lord Provost of Edinburgh among the Directors, Sir James Falshaw having been successful in the recent elections. Born in Leeds in 1819, he became a civil engineer, and from 1845, when he moved to Scotland, he was associated with the construction of various railways in Scotland. During his term of office he was associated with the widening of the North Bridge, among other major public works. In 1877 he retired from public life, but remained on the Boards of several Scottish railways and was Chairman of the NBR. He also took part in the inquiry into the Tay Bridge Disaster in 1879, and died on 14th June, 1889.

The revenue for the first half year of £5,300 1s. 11d. enabled a 2 per cent dividend, slightly less than forecast, to be declared. Traffic receipts for August were also encouraging:

	£	s.	d.
Goods and Minerals	117	11	4
Passengers	182	9	8

On the other hand, the SIC had threatened to withdraw the water supply from Roslin, and the NBR, no doubt exasperated at the Board's indecision, insisted on acceptance of the Roslin water company's offer of £20 per year. This was agreed by the Board, thus bringing the matter to an end.

Sir James Falshaw 1874-1877, Bart., and Lord Provost of Edinburgh.

Chapter Four

Extension and Amalgamation

With the line open at last for all traffic, at least as far as Roslin, a joint committee was set up with the NBR. In the event, only one meeting was ever held, on Monday 29th March, 1875, chaired by John Stirling, the NBR Chairman. Little business appears to have been discussed, apart from the authorisation of sidings to serve Gilmerton Colliery, to be installed at the expense of the Glasgow Iron Company. It was noted that the ELR had received capital for the extension line as follows:

Shotts Iron Co.	£10,000
Waddell	£5,000
ELR Directors	£500
	£15,500

The NBR agreed to consider assisting the Board in the shortfall of £6,000.

At the tenth half-yearly meeting held two days later, the shareholders learnt that a dividend of 2½ per cent would be paid. Instead of a larger amount, the Directors had paid back some of the interest on the overdraft, and stated that the overdraft would be paid back by using any capital remaining after the extension had been completed. The extension had not been proceeded with, due to the capital not having been fully subscribed. It was announced that the Shotts Iron Co. was investing 'up to £10,000' in the Mauricewood and Greenlaw areas, in anticipation of the extension of the line. Within a week of the meeting the NBR confirmed the contribution of the necessary £6,000, which would be included in the North British Railway (Additional Powers Act), 1876, which was passed on 13th July, 1876.

A letter of resignation was received on 7th April from Lord Provost Falshaw, as he had become a Director of the NBR. A Mr Cassels, of Glasgow, was appointed in his place. Timetable cards were to be printed and distrubuted in local hotels; regrettably, none of these appear to have survived.

A quiet period followed, during which the passenger figures rose steadily, with a total of 21,049 tickets sold from the three stations between February and July 1875. Similar increases were recorded in goods and mineral traffic:

	Gilmerton	Loanhead	Roslin	Total
Goods	579	1,591	1,882	4,052
Minerals	3,025	733	869	4,627
Coal	187	846	318	1,351
Totals	3,791	3,170	3,069	10,030

(All figures in tons)

The healthy goods figure for Roslin may be explained by the traffic consigned to the contractor and other local businesses in connection with the Glencorse extension, as they were never to reach such high figures again, apart from a short-lived period in 1880-1881.

EDINBURGH, LOANHEAD, and ROSLIN RAILWAY.
Up Trains.

Stations and Sidings.		Distance from Edinburgh.		1 Roslin Goods	2 Pass. 1 2 4 Class	3	4 Pass. 1 2 4 Class	5	6 Roslin Goods	7	8 Pass. 1 2 4 Class	9	10 Pass. 1 2 4 Class	
		Miles.	Chains	a.m.	a.m.		p.m.		p.m.		p.m.		p.m.	
Edinburgh	... dep.	...	...	...	10 20	...	1 17	...	...	...	4 2	...	8 20	...
Leith Walk	... „													
Portobello	... arr.	3	0	......	10 28	...	1 25	...	...	...	4 10	...	8 28	......
Do.	... dep.	3	0	...	10 29	......	1 26	......	12 15	......	4 11	......	8 29	......
Niddrie Junction	... arr.	4	33	......	10 33	......	1 49	......	12 25	......	4 14	......	8 33	......
Do.	... dep.	4	33		...	...	...	...	12 39	...	...	...	...	
Millerhill Junction	... arr.	6	19	......	10 37	......	1 34	...	12 45	...	4 19	......	8 37	......
Millerhill Junction dep.		6	19	7 40	10 38	...	1 35	...	12 55	...	4 20	......	8 38	......
Gilmerton	... „	8	43	7 50	10 44	......	1 41	......	1 5	......	4 26	......	8 44	......
Edgefield Quarry Siding	„	...	...	7 55	...	......	......	......	1 10	......	...	......	......	......
Edgefield Siding	... „			8 0	......	......	......	......	1 15	......	......	......	......	......
Ramsay Pit	... „	10	18	8 10	...	...	...	...	1 25	...	...	...	...	
Loanhead	... „	10	39	8 41	10 49	......	1 46	......	2 40	......	4 31	......	8 49	......
Roslin	... arr.	12	12	8 50	10 58	...	1 55	...	2 50	...	4 40	...	8 58	...

NOTES.

The Passenger Trains all run through from Edinburgh.

No. 1.—*Shunts at Loanhead for No. 1 Down Passenger.* If necessary, Engine must run from Millerhill to Loanhead with Train Staff should the Train be late.

No. 6.—*Shunts at Loanhead for Nos. 4 Up and 6 Down Passenger trains.* Performs its shunting work and weighs Shotts Coal and Char Traffic at Loanhead before going to Roslin.

Down Trains.

Stations and Sidings.		Distance from Roslin.		1 Pass. 1 2 4 Class	2 Roslin Goods	3	4 Pass. 1 2 4 Class	5	6 Pass. 1 2 4 Class	7	8 Roslin Goods	9 Pass. 1 2 4 Class	10	11	12
		Miles.	Chains	a.m.	a.m.		p.m.		p.m.		p.m.	p.m.			
Roslin	... dep.	...	...	8 35	9 0	...	12 15	...	2 30	...	3 5	6 40	...	...	
Boroughlee Siding	... „	1	19		9 15	......	......	......	......	......	......	......	......	......	
Loanhead	... „	1	53	8 40	9 25	...	12 20	...	2 35	...	3 30	6 45	...	...	
Ramsay Pit	... „	1	74		9 35	...									
Edgefield Siding	... „	...	...		9 45	...									
Gilmerton	... „	3	49	8 45	9 55	......	12 25	......	2 40	......		6 50	......	......	
Millerhill Junction arr.		5	73	8 51	10 5	......	12 31	......	2 46	......	3 50	6 56	......	......	
Millerhill Junction ... dep.		5	73	8 53	10 6	......	12 33	......	2 48	......	4 16	6 58	......	......	
Niddrie Junction	... arr.	7	59		10 14	...	12 37	...	2 52	...	4 23	7 2	...	...	
Do. do.	... dep.	7	59	8 57	10 40	......	......	......	...	...	4 35	......	......	......	
Portobello	... arr.	9	12	9 3	10 45	......	12 43	......	2 58	......	4 45	7 8	......	......	
Do.	... dep.	9	12	9 5	...	...	12 45	...	3 0	......		7 10	......	......	
Leith Walk	... arr.				Stop	...	...	...	...	...	stop.	...	...	...	
Edinburgh	... „	12	12	9 15	......	......	12 55	...	3 10	......	......	7 20	......	......	

NOTES.

The Passenger Trains all run through to Edinburgh.

The report of the next half-yearly meeting, on 30th September, 1874, contained the, by now, customary statement regarding repayment of the interest on the overdraft, which again reduced the dividend to 2½ per cent. A completion date for the extension was given as March or April 1876, which was as inaccurate as those given in the past. (This referred only to Railway No. 1, i.e. Roslin-Glencorse.)

The next six-month period appears to have been even quieter than the last, with the extension proceeding much slower than had been hoped, due to bad weather. A claim by a Mrs Cochrane for the loss of her turnip crop was paid, the lady receiving ten guineas in compensation. It would have been interesting to learn how the loss occurred, but details are, unfortunately, not recorded.

By February 1876, the track bed and rails had been completed to just short of the viaduct, and the station site had been excavated. Points had been installed for the short branch to the Moat Colliery at Roslin, but the owners, the Glasgow Iron Co., appeared reluctant to finalise the signalling arrangements and this was left in abeyance meantime. The progress prompted Waddell to ask Bouch's office for details of the 'Mineral Extension No. 2' as he was 'anxious to proceed with railway No. 2, and request plans and sections of the branch - sections would do in the meantime so that I can get the line formed', he wrote on 7th March. Evidently he did not receive a prompt reply, as he wrote again on 25th: 'The farmer is pressing me to get it (the line) fenced before he begins to sow, besides I will soon be idle with the exception of one cutting and my horses are all standing in the stables for want of work'. The cutting referred to was that from the west end of the viaduct to the site of Glencorse station. This had to be left until the viaduct had been completed, to allow the estimated 8,000 cubic yards of spoil to be carried across and used to form the eastern approach embankment. At this date only the piers were finished, with the first set of wooden centreing in position to form the arches. All of the bridges between Roslin and the site of this embankment were complete, and the track laid and ballasted.

It was not until July that the tender for Greenlaw (as it was referred to at this time) station buildings was accepted from Mr Tait, a local builder from Penicuik. His quote of £305 was for the erection of a station building and a 'dwelling house'. He also built the signal box, but his price is not recorded in any of the minutes. The station was to be in the same style as Loanhead, rather than the grander design at Roslin, which was altogether a poor affair, hardly befitting the status of the terminus of a railway company. No doubt, all such ideas had disappeared from the minds of the Directors, along with most of the capital.

Bouch's report, submitted to the half-yearly meeting on 29th September, 1876, confirmed that the viaduct was complete, with the exception of the parapet and handrails. The cutting mentioned previously had not been started, but work was progressing on the station. A further 3 ton crane and a weighing machine had been ordered, and agreement had been reached with the Glasgow Iron Co. over the signalling of its branch.

A complaint was received on 23rd October from the solicitors acting for the Glencorse School Board. The school was sited next to the main road into Glencorse, and it had been necessary to purchase part of the property to take the line under the road at this point. Evidently, the new boundary wall was not high enough, and had to be heightened, and broken glass put on top - a practice which would not be permissible today.

November saw Waddell asking the NBR to provide points and crossings for Greenlaw, to plans prepared by Bouch's assistant, Trimble. The NBR insisted that these would be made from steel, not wrought iron as had been estimated for, thereby increasing the cost. The NBR was not taking any chances with the BoT inspector, after its experiences at Loanhead.

A site meeting was necessary to solve a problem which arose in January 1877 over the level crossing of the road leading to Eastfield farm, as the line continued on to reach Eastfield Colliery. The original plan was to have included an overbridge, but the ELR suggested that a level crossing was all that was necessary. The meeting took place on 25th, with Walker, the NBR Secretary, James Bell, the NBR Engineer, and Trimble attending. Despite the presence of so many high-powered attendees, the decision was deferred until a later date.

Trimble must have been pressing for completion of the station buildings, as Tait wrote on 1st March, reporting that the plaster on the walls was not dry, and that he had laid the floors, but would 'not be responsible for them'. As well as building the signal box, he would also attend to the nameboard, which would read 'Glencorse'. This is interesting as the controversy surrounding the name did not surface until July, after the opening, when John Inglis of Glencorse, Lord Justice General and Lord President of the Court of Session (who resided nearby), decided on Glencorse, rather than Glencross, which was used internally by the NBR. The use of Greenlaw, of course, led to confusion with its counterpart in Berwickshire, which had opened as part of the Berwickshire Railway in November 1863.

Once again, bad weather was to delay the contractor over the winter, as can be seen from the Directors' report dated 30th March, 1877. This also announced the conclusion of the agreement to amalgamate with the NBR, from 31st July, for a dividend of 4½ per cent for the year to 31st July, 1878, and 5 per cent thereafter. The Amalgamation Bill was before Parliament, and was expected to become law in May. (The Royal Assent was gained on 28th June, 1877.)

By the second week of May, the extension was ready for inspection at last, and the Secretary wrote to the BoT on 8th May informing them that the extension line would be available for that purpose from 9th May. Major-General Hutchinson was directed to inspect the line by a minute dated the 9th, but the ELR had to wait until the 12th, when he telegraphed them: 'I propose to inspect the extension of the ELR on Wednesday 16th, starting at 9.00 from the Waverley. Please have ready an undertaking as to the method of working the extended portion. I do not see how a turntable at Roslin will enable you to turn the engines at Glencross, which appears to be the passenger terminus of the line.'

The ELR Board appear to have overlooked the problems which had arisen regarding the method of working the line which delayed the opening in 1874, as they again did not provide such an undertaking in advance of the inspection.

It is clear from Hutchinson's message that he had realised that, while the turntable had been correctly sited when Roslin was the terminus, it was now situated in the wrong place. From the content of his inspection report, he must have been given the impression that the line would be extended to Penicuik for passenger traffic, as he states, 'There is an engine turntable at Roslin, and looking to the probability of the early extension to Penicuik, it is not thought worthwhile moving it to Glencorse. In the meantime, no engine shall run tender first between

Roslin and Edinburgh.' There was, of course, no intention of extending the passenger service, and the turntable remained where it was for another 56 years.

As to the rest of the inspector's findings, the ELR must have been reminded of the 1874 inspection as, once again, the bridges and the Glencorse viaduct were commended, but the trackwork and signalling came in for criticism.

Roslin Station
The only requirement here concerned the engine shed, which was accessed directly from the main line. To avoid a facing point on a running line, Hutchison required that the siding points be moved to the loop line.

Glasgow Iron Company's Junction
A small signal cabin of this name had been provided to control entry to Roslin Colliery, although the main line signals were normally left at clear unless a train required access to the sidings. As the line was on a 1 in 66 gradient falling towards the station at this point, the inspector required that the points be set for the goods yard when trains were working at the sidings. He made two suggestions, that either the siding be brought back through the overbridge (which would have had to be extended over the additional track) and connected to the new engine shed road, or that means had to be provided to ensure that the goods yard points would be locked in the position outlined. Naturally, the ELR did not think much of his first suggestion, due to the cost of altering the bridge 'merely to see our points and train'.

Glencorse Station
The layout at the terminus was approved, apart from some interlocking of two signal levers and the points requiring double connecting rods. A check rail was also required at the 15 chain curve where the line joined the viaduct.

He also remarked on the lack of block instruments and the undertaking to work the line by Train Staff and Ticket, combined with the Block Telegraph. This time, he also insisted that the undertaking must be signed both by the ELR and the NBR, as the working company.

In conclusion, Hutchinson stated:

Pending completion of the above named requirements and the receipt of the undertakings I must report that by reason of the incompletion of the works the extension of the Edinburgh, Loanhead and Roslin Railway from Roslin to Glencorse cannot be opened for passenger traffic without danger to the public using the line.'

In consequence, the BoT informed the ELR on 18th May that the opening must be posponed for one month, to allow the company to comply. Also on the 18th the BoT received a letter from Mr Henderson, of Milton Farm, Milton Bridge expressing his concern at the lack of visibility at the level crossing where the public right of way crossed the railway on his land. The crossing, which was in a cutting and on a curve, was used by children attending Glencorse school, and the visibility was less than 200 yards in each direction. He stated also that the contractor had wished to put in a footbridge, but that this had been overruled by the ELR on cost grounds.

In their reply the BoT had to point out that, as the crossing was not a 'public carriage road', they had no power to compel the railway company to provide a bridge, but they promised to 'point out the desirability of a bridge being substituted for this level crossing.' This recommendation was conveyed to the company on the same day.

Two days later, the undertakings were forwarded, and a re-inspection was arranged for 25th June. This visit by Major Hutchinson proved to be more successful, as the problem over access to the colliery at Roslin had been solved by chaining together the two sets of keys which worked the goods yard and the colliery connection points. The ELR undertook also to provide a footbridge on the right of way 'within the course of one month', which assurance proved satisfactory to the BoT.

On 28th June the Secretary finally received the Board's minute No. R5386, which stated that 'the B of T see no objection to the opening of the Extension Rly for public traffic on condition that it shall be worked in accordance with the undertakings'.

At last, the shareholders could see their line fully open for all traffic, with the exception of the mineral extension although, with the impending amalgamation, the days of the ELR as an independent company were soon to be over.

April 1880.

ROSLIN BRANCH and GLENCORSE EXTENSION.

WEEK-DAYS.

Up Trains. Stations and Sidings.	Distance from Edinburgh.	1 Roslin Goods	2	3 Roslin Goods	4 Pass. 1 2 3 Class.	5 Roslin Goods	6 Pass. 1 2 3 Class	7	8 Pass. 1 2 3 Class	9 Pass. 1 2 3 Class.	10 Pass. 1 2 3 Class
	Miles. Chains	a.m.		a.m.	a.m.	a.m	p.m.		p.m.	p.m.	p.m.
Edinburgh ... ... dep,		...	...	...	9 52	...	.1 17	...	4 35	6 15	9 0
Leith Walk ... ,,		...		...							...
Portobello ... ... arr.	3 0	...	...	9 59	...	1 25	...	4 43	6 24	9 8	...
Do. ... ... dep.	3 0	5 0	...	10 0	11 30	1 26	...	4 44	6 25	9 9	......
Niddrie Junction ... arr.	4 33	5 5		......	11 35						
Do. ... ... dep.	4 33	5 8	......	10 3	11 45						
Millerhill Junction ... arr.	6 19	5 15		10 7	11 51	1 34		4 47	6 48	9 11	
Millerhill Junction dep.	6 19	5 40		7 30	10 10	12 20	1 35	...	4 52	6 32	9 17
Gilmerton . ... ,,	8 43	5 50	......	7 40	10 16	12 30	1 41	......	4 53	6 35	9 18
Straiton Siding ... ,,		6 0	......	7 50	......	12 35	...	......	4 59	6 41	9 24
Edgefield Quarry Siding ,,						12 40			...	...	...
Edgefield Siding ... ,,			......	......	....	12 45	...		......	......	......
Ramsay Pit ... ,,	10 18					12 50					
Loanhead ... ... ,,	10 39	6 10	......	8 15	10 21	1 10	1 46	......	5 4	6 46	9 29
Roslin ... ... ,,	12 12	Stop.	...	8 21	10 28	1 20	1 53	...	5 11	6 53	9 36
Glencorse ... ... arr.	14 18	......	......	Stop.	10 35	1 30	2 0	...	5 18	7 0	9 43

NOTES.

No. 4.—Detaches Polton portion at Millerhill. Engine does shunting at Glencorse between 10-35 and 11-20 a.m.
Nos. 4, 6, 8, and 10 Trains run through from Edinburgh.
No. 9.—Passengers for Gilmerton, Loanhead, Roslin, and Glencorse change at Millerhill.
Glasgow Iron Coy.'s Siding, Roslin.—No. 5 Train works this Siding daily, in terms of General Manager's Circular, M.670, dated 27th June 1877

WEEK-DAYS.

Down Trains, Stations and Sidings.	Distance from Glencorse.	1 Roslin Goods	2	3 Pass. 1 2 3 Class	4 Roslin Goods	5 Pass. 1 2 3 Class.	6 Pass. 1 2 3 Class.	7 Roslin Goods	8 Pass. 1 2 3 Class.	9 Pass. 1 2 3 Class	10	11	12
	Miles. Chains	a.m.		a.m.	a.m.	a.m.	p.m.	p.m.	p.m.	p.m.			
Glencorse ... ... dep.		......	......	8 35	...	11 20	2 25	2 30	5 40	7 15	......	......	
Roslin ... ... ,,	2 1	......	...	8 40	8 45	11 25	2 30	2 40	5 45	7 20	...	......	
Boroughlee Siding ... ,,	3 20	......	......	......	8 55	......	......	2 47	......	......	......	......	
Loanhead ... ... ,,	3 54	6 45	...	8 44	9 15	11 30	2 35	3 10	5 50	7 24	...	......	
Ramsay Pit ... ,,	3 75	......	......	......	9 20	...	...	......	......	......			
Edgefield Siding ... ,,		...	...	......	9 30	...	...	...	...	...	...		
Straiton Siding ... ,,		......	......	6 55	9 35	...	...	3 20	......	......			
Gilmerton ... ,,	5 50	......	...	7 5	8 49	9 45	11 35	2 40	3 25	5 55	7 29	......	
Millerhill Junction arr.	7 74	......	...	7 15	8 54	9 55	11 41	2 46	3 35	6 1	7 34	......	
Millerhill Junction ... dep.	7 74	......	......	......	8 57	10 0	11 43	2 48	3 50	6 6	7 35	......	
Niddrie Junction ... arr.	9 60	Stop.	...	......	10 8	...	...	3 55	......	......			
Do. do. ... dep.	9 60	......	...	......	10 40	......	...	3 57	......	......			
Portobello ... ... arr.	11 18	......	...	......	9 3	10 45	11 53	2 58	4 2	6 16	7 43	......	
Do. ... ... dep.	11 18	......	...	......	9 5	......	11 55	3 0	...	6 17	7 45	......	
Leith Walk ... arr.		...	...	......		......	...	...	Stop.	...	......		
Edinburgh ,,	14 18	......	...	......	9 14	......	12 5	3 10	......	6 27	7 55	......	

Nos. 3, 5, 6, and 9 Trains run through to Edinburgh.
No. 3.—Attaches Polton portion at Millerhill.
No. 8.—Passengers from Glencorse, Roslin, Loanhead, and Gilmerton change at Millerhill.

Working Timetable of the branch to Glencorse, 1880.

Chapter Five

Part of the NBR
1877-1922

With amalgamation into the NBR, the branch became one of the many lines feeding Scotland's largest railway company. The NBR Directors would have found their new acquisition profitable, when the new sources of traffic establishing themselves in the late 1870s were added to those already using the line.

The NBR siding register for 1877 shows the following industries connected to the branch, each with their own private siding:

Straiton Oil and Lime Works siding	Straiton Estate Co.
Edgefield Quarry siding	Mr Waddell
Edgefield Weighs siding	Shotts Iron Co.
Ramsey Pit	Shotts Iron Co.
Boroughlee Colliery	Shotts Iron Co.
Moat Colliery	Glasgow Iron Co.
Glencross	Shotts Iron Co.

It will be noted that the 'official' names used in this list differ in some cases from those used elsewhere, e.g. Moat for Roslin, and Glencross instead of Glencorse. Edgefield Weighs siding was in fact the north connection to the Ramsey pit, but is listed separately, as it was controlled by a small signal box, described in Chapter Twelve. The contractor evidently used the sandstone quarry at Edgefield for some time after his contract had finished, but it had disappeared from the 1889 edition of the siding register. Gilmerton Colliery is not listed in the 1877 edition, as it was still under construction.

The industries on the mineral extension are also missing from the register, as this opened in the latter part of 1877. With the extension open for traffic, it is a suitable point to review the mining operations and industries it served.

As was described in Chapter One, Greenlaw pit had been in existence since the 1840s, but the Shotts Iron Co. had decided to sink a new pit at Eastfield, some distance to the south, in 1875. After boring to a depth of only 84 feet, the operation had to be abandoned, due to unforeseen flooding. Having invested heavily in the area (and encouraged the construction of the ELR), attention turned to Mauricewood, to the north-west, at a higher level. Ironstone was known to outcrop here, with coal seams below. The original Greenlaw site was also redeveloped at the same time.

By 1876, 300 men were employed, with ironstone the main product, and the SIC was anxious for the railway to be extended, as the output was transported by road to Kevock siding, on the Esk Valley Railway, as per the NBR agreement. To provide housing for the many miners who had moved from Lanarkshire, the company had built 49 cottages a short distance south of Eastfield, near Penicuik, which are known collectively as Shottstown to this day.

After the mineral railway opened, a self-acting incline was constructed from Mauricewood down to sidings south of Glencorse station. Greenlaw was served by a siding immediately behind the station itself.

An early view of Glencorse, taken from the hill to the north-west, shows that 0-6-0 tender locomotives were used occasionally on passenger trains. *Alan Maclaren*

The road side of Roslin station is visible in the background of this Victorian photograph, with the station house to its right. *George Campbell*

The Penicuik Gas Company opened on 30th June, 1878, served by a siding on the up side. As it was not a passenger line, a wooden scotch block was used, rather than a catch point, to divert runaway wagons from the main line.

Between 1877 and 1881 the ironstone was calcinated, i.e. burnt to remove impurities, in open hearths at Mauricewood. This reduced the weight (and transport costs) considerably, but incurred the displeasure of the local landowners, who raised court actions on the grounds of the damage which the resultant fumes caused to their trees. Burning was restricted to the months of November, December and January, but the SIC had to stop altogether in 1880, after an action was instituted by Lord President Inglis to prevent the company burning at any time, which was upheld, despite an appeal to the House of Lords. Eventually, new hearths were built at Shotts, Lanarkshire, and the ironstone which had accumulated during the dispute boosted the branch's traffic figures for 1881.

The hazards faced by the men and boys working underground were looked upon as part of the job, included amongst which should be mentioned fires at Mauricewood in 1886, which took four days to subdue, and one the next year at Burghlee, which was extinguished only after 14 weeks by flooding part of the coal workings. These were subsequently abandoned, reducing the output by three-quarters. At least, these types of incident led only to loss of earnings, whereas the the fire which started at Mauricewood on 5th September, 1889 led to the deaths of 63 workers and closed the pit for 18 months.

Such was the density of the fire and the attendant roof falls, that the last of the bodies were not recovered until the end of March 1890. Reconstruction was completed 12 months later, utilising a safer method of pumping the water out of the workings. It had been found that the fire had spread rapidly, due to the fact that the pipes carrying steam to the underground pumping engine had dried out the many timber supports used in the workings. The new system used a set of pumps on the surface, which drove similar pumps at the foot of the workings by hydraulic (water) pressure. Coal as well as ironstone was now mined, also being sold locally at the pit head.

The re-opening of Mauricewood, regretfully, was short-lived as, when another underground fire broke out in February 1897, the SIC finally decided to abandon operations in the area (Greenlaw had closed in 1889), and concentrate at Loanhead. Other reasons for closure included the cost of underground haulage, which used pit ponies, and the availability of cheap ore imported from Spain.

Following the closure of Greenlaw, one other attempt was made to revive the site at Eastfield, despite the earlier setbacks. This attempt reached 360 feet before it became clear that the flooding was beyond the capacity of the extra pumps which had been brought in.

Eastfield then became a coal depot, initially run by the SIC, instead of being the centre of a thriving mining area. The SIC's maintenance workshop and sawmill were also established on the site. As the end of the century drew near, it can be seen that most of the reasons for the construction of the extension had disappeared, leaving the moderate passenger traffic as far as Glencorse as the main source of revenue south of Roslin.

July 1896.

ROSLIN BRANCH and GLENCORSE EXTENSION.

WEEK-DAYS.

Up Trains.

Stations and Sidings.	Distance from Edinburgh (Miles)	(Chains)	1 Roslin Goods	2 From Niddrie West	3 Portobello and Glencorse	4 Pass. 1 3 Class.	5 Roslin Goods	6 Portobello and Glencorse	7 Stores Thurs July 30	8 Pass. ex. Sat. 1 3 Class.	9 Pass. Sat. only. 1 3 Class.	10 Portobello and Glencorse	11 Pass. 1 3 Class	12 Pass. 1 3 Class.	13 Pass. 1 3 Class.	14 Pass. Sat. only. 1 3 Class.
			a.m.		Min.	a.m. 9 50	a.m.		Min.	p.m.	p.m.	Min.	p.m.	p.m.	p.m.	p.m.
Edinburgh ...dep.						9 50		p.m.	p.m.	1 30	2 0		4 47	...	9 0	11 0
Portobello ... ,,	3	0				8 0	9 58			1 38	2 9		4 55	...	9 8	11 8
Niddrie South Junc... arr.	4	33														
Do. ... ... dep.	4	33				8 5	10 1			1 41			4 58	...	9 11	11 12
Millerhill Junc. ... arr.	4	66				8 10	10 4			1 44	2 15		5 1	...	9 14	11 16
— Millerhill Jc. dep.	6	19	7 20			8 50	10 5	11 55	12 30	1 25	1 48	2 19	3 50	5 2	6 40	9 15	11 20
Gilmerton ... ,,	8	48	7 30			8 57	10 11	12 3	12 40	1 34	1 54	2 25	4 0	5 8	6 47	9 21	11 27
Straiton Siding ,,	9	57	7 35			9 10			12 15	1 5			4 30				
Edgefield Sidings ,,	9	78				9 20			12 20	1 15			4 40				
Loanhead ... arr.	10	39	8 0			9 25	10 15	12 25	1 20	1 40	1 58	2 29	4 45	5 12	6 52	9 25	11 32
— Do. ... ... dep.	10	39	8 10			9 30	10 16	12 30	Stop.	2 4	1 59	2 30	Stop.	5 13	6 53	9 26	11 33
Burghlee Siding ,,	10	78							12 40								
— Roslin ... ... arr.	12	12	8 20			9 36	10 20	12 45		2 10	2 3	2 34		5 17	6 57	9 30	11 37
— Do. ... ... dep.	12	12	Stop.			9 45	10 21	12 50		2 11	2 4	2 35		5 18	6 59	9 31	11 39
— Glencorse ... arr.	14	13				9 50	10 25	12 55		2 15	2 8	2 39		5 22	7 3	9 35	11 43

No. 3.—*Meets at Loanhead No. 2 Down.*

No. 4.—*Meets at Loanhead No. 2 Down.*

No. 5.—Takes Road Wagon ticketed "Edinburgh and Roslin Road Wagon," the Van Way-bills to be delivered to Station Master, Roslin. Calls at Gilmerton and Edgefield Sidings only to leave Road Van Goods.

No. 7.—*Shunts at Loanhead for Passenger Train.*

No. 8.—Is detached from Penicuik portion at Millerhill daily except Saturdays.

No. 9.—Is detached from Polton Train at Millerhill.

No. 14.—Is detached from Polton Train at Millerhill.

Edgefield Sidings.—These Sidings are worked by Up Trains only. (No. M—1340, 5th March 1883.)

WEEK-DAYS.

Down Trains.

Stations and Sidings.	1 Pass. 1 3 Class.	2 Roslin Goods	3 Portobello and Glencorse	4 Pass. 1 3 Class	5 Roslin Goods	6 Portobello and Glencorse	7 Stores Thurs July 30	8 Pass. ex. Sat. 1 3 Class	9 Pass. Sat. only. 1 3 Class.	10 Roslin Goods	11 Pass. Sat. only. 1 3 Class.	12 Portobello and Glencorse	13 Pass. 1 3 Class.	14 Pass. 1 3 Class.	15 Pass. Sat. only. 1 3 Class.
	a.m.	a.m.	a.m.	a.m.	p.m.	Sat. only. Min.	Ex. Sat. p.m.	p.m.	p.m.	p.m.	Min.		p.m.	p.m.	p.m.
— Glencorse ... dep.	8 30		10 30	11 10	1 20		2 17	2 25		3 25			6 10	7 25	10 0
— Roslin ... arr.	8 34		10 35	11 14	1 25			2 29		3 29			6 14	7 29	10 4
— Do. ... ... dep.	8 35	8 40	10 40	11 15	1 30			2 30		3 30			6 15	7 30	10 6
Burghlee Siding ,,		9 10	10 52		1 45										
— Loanhead ... arr.	8 38	9 13	10 55	11 19	1 50			2 34		3 34			6 19	7 34	10 9
— Do. ... ... dep.	8 39	10 20	11 30	11 20	Stop.	1 45	2 0	2 35	2 45	3 35	5 20	6 20	7 35	10 10
Straiton Siding ,,		10 30	11 40				2 0	2 15		3 5		5 45			
Gilmerton ... ,,	8 44	10 41 45	11 25					2 40	3 20	3 40	5 55	6 25	7 40	10 15
— Millerhill Jc.... arr.	8 48	10 50	11 55	11 30		2 10	2 25	2 32	2 45	3 25	3 45	6 0	6 30	7 45	10 20
Millerhill Jc. ... dep.	8 52			11 34					2 46		4 15	3 46	6 10	7 46	10 24
Niddrie South Junc. arr.		Stop.	Stop.			Stop.	Stop.								
Do. do. ... dep.	8 55			11 37					2 49	4 20			6 15	7 49	10 28
Portobello ... ,,	9 0			11 41					2 53	4 25	3 53	6 20	7 53	10 32
Piersbill ... ,,															
Abbeyhill ... ,,															
St Margarets ... ,,										Stop.	Stop.				
Edinburgh ... ,,	9 8			11 49					3 1	4 1			8 1	10 40

No. 1.—Is attached to Polton Train at Millerhill.

No. 3.—Takes Shotts Traffic to Millerhill. *Shunts at Loanhead for No. 4 Down.*

No. 4.—Attaches Dalkeith Train at Millerhill.

No. 5.—When necessary makes Cross Trip from Loanhead to Roslin, working Burghlee Siding.

No. 7.—Takes to Millerhill Oil Tanks from Straiton for Whifflet.

No. 15.—Is attached to Polton Train at Millerhill.

Working Timetable for the Glencorse branch, July 1896.

The staff at Glencorse pose for the photographer in NBR days. In the background the fireman of the 0-4-4T has taken advantage of the situation to clean the locomotive's smokebox.

Jim Page Collection

Loanhead station staff pose for the camera, sometime after 1895, as the extension, added at that time, can be seen on the right. The poster on the left advertises the 'direct route' to Aberdeen, via the Forth and Tay bridges. *Midlothian Council Local Studies Department*

A 19th century view of Ramsey Colliery, taken from one of the houses in Station Road, with a selection of dumb-buffered wagons visible. The platform fence and trespass notice can just be seen in the centre foreground.   *Alan McLaren Collection*

A 19th century view of Ramsey Colliery, showing the boilers for the winding engine, and the pithead gear.   *Alan Maclaren*

Main Street, Roslin, looking north, at the turn of the century. The road rises towards the railway overbridge in the centre background.   *Midlothian Council Local Studies Department*

The opposition wait at Roslin to return to Edinburgh. Two horse buses can be seen, one for each of the hotels. A one shilling fare is advertised by the bus outside the Original Hotel.
                                        Midlothian Council Local Studies Department

Glencorse Barracks

The present Infantry training Depot, which is sited immediately opposite the site of Glencorse station, had been established to house prisoners from the Napoleonic Wars but, by the 1870s, had become disused. The coming of the railway produced a change of emphasis, with the establishment of a base for the Edinburgh County Militia, a form of Territorial Regiment. The movement of the permanent staff from Dalkeith, where they had been based, to Glencorse on 19th March, 1878 was the forerunner of many troop trains which would be run over the branch over the next 81 years.

Bilston Glen Viaduct

By the late 1880s, subsidence in the area of Bilston Glen was causing concern to local landowners, and the viaduct appeared to be settling slightly, into the bargain. Ever since the loss of the Tay Bridge in 1879, problems with any structure having connections with Sir Thomas Bouch were viewed with particular concern by the NBR Board and, accordingly, an investigation was authorised and carried out in 1890.

Where railway lines were liable to subsidence caused by mining operations, the usual practice was to agree with the relevant mining company on the siting of a suitable 'pillar' of coal which would be left untouched underground, thus minimising any tendency to settlement. In this case the nearest workings were 350 yards away, but an underground roadway had been driven to within 50 yards of the branch. If the company were to protect the viaduct from future workings, its consulting engineer estimated that 140 acres would be required, and that the cost could be as much as £150,000, at the then current rate of £1,070 per acre.

The NBR Engineer's report showed that the abutments had settled slightly, and accordingly he recommended that metal straps should be fitted to retain the stonework. The brick piers on the other hand, showed no sign of settlement. Under the circumstances, the company took the unusual step of proposing to replace the entire structure with an embankment. Accordingly, a Parliamentary application was made to revive compulsory powers, under the Regulation of Railways Act of 1842, to aquire the land necessary to build the embankment. This was vigorously opposed by the local landowner, Lt Col Trotter, one of the original ELR Directors, who maintained that the Glen would be spoilt if the viaduct was replaced. His nearby house, Drydenbank, had suddenly collapsed some years previously, and the resulting court case with the Shotts Iron Co. had eventually gone to the House of Lords, on appeal.

The Board of Trade were instructed to report on the situation, and Major Marindin issued his report on 13th August, 1890. The parties involved had met in Edinburgh on Friday 27th and Saturday 28th June, with a visit thereafter to the viaduct and the surrounding area taking place on the Friday evening. The Major was shown the structure and the repairs to the abutments, and he commented on the 'first class' brickwork forming the piers. He agreed that the surroundings were beautiful, and was shown the remains of Drydenbank, some ¼ mile away.

Mr Asher, QC, for the NBR stated in evidence that the company was worried by the subsidence, and by the size of the pillar of coal, but thought that an embankment would be a better idea. He gave the cost of constructing the embankment at £15,000-£16,000, and suggested that it would not 'injure the property'.

Col Trotter had assembled a team of mining and railway engineers to support his case. Damage to property was estimated at £5,000, and the beauty of the Glen would be destroyed. In their opinion, only 16 acres of coal would be sufficent to secure the viaduct's continued stability.

In a further statement Mr Asher conceded that the beauty of the Glen would be destroyed, but Col Trotter would be paid for it (!) and, although the area had residential value, he did not live there now.

During his summing up, Major Marindin reviewed the coal workings in the vicinity of the viaduct, which ran north/south, in relation to the coal seams passing diagonally across from north-east to south-west. The depth of the Great Seam was about 140 fathoms at the north end and 225 fathoms at the south end. The Major decided that 24 acres would be adequate to safeguard the existing viaduct, at a cost of £25,670. If the NBR applied for an Act of Parliament to construct an embankment, the SIC would not be able to work coal within 250 yards of the structure until a decision had been made. The Shotts company would have been able to claim compensation from the railway company for loss of production during this period. After considering all of the options available, the NBR decided that replacement of the existing viaduct would be the cheapest solution.

The design finally approved was for a single main span 330 ft long x 40 ft deep, with one 56 ft span at each end. Two new piers were required, each consisting of a concrete base reinforced by old rails, supplied by the railway company, supporting an ashlar pier with a granite coping to take the expansion bearings. The piers rested on firm sandstone, 20 ft below ground level on the north side, 25 ft on the south, while the outer ends of the side spans were to be supported by granite abutments.

Messrs P. & W. MacLellan of Glasgow carried out the work of replacing the original structure, commencing on Sunday 15th May, 1892, when the first of the girders was successfully removed. The complete renewal of the structure was achieved in the remarkably short period of 11 days, without incident. During the renewal, train services were terminated at Loanhead, the 9.50 am from Waverley being the first to traverse the new bridge on Thursday 26th May.

Ever since its construction, the bridge has attracted generations of those local youngsters brave enough to cross the glen by using the lower member of the main span, particularly during the passage of a train, an act of 'derring do' as foolhardy as it is spectacular.

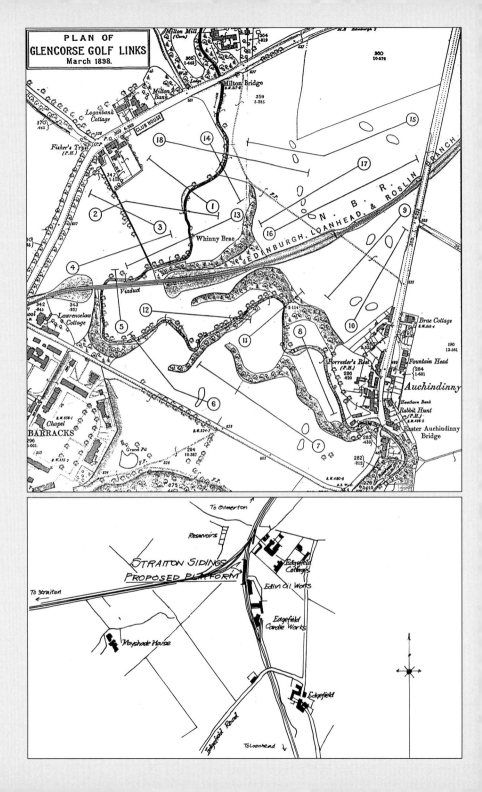

Other Events

By 1894, the station accommodation at Loanhead had become inadequate, and plans were prepared for an extension to the station building. The existing booking office was enlarged, with a new entrance porch and booking hall with double doors giving access to the platform. A general waiting room was included, allowing the provision of 1st and 3rd class ladies' waiting rooms. The new building, which was also provided with a platform canopy, was brought into use early in 1895. Ironically, this later extension outlived the original building and is still in existence at the time of writing.

It appears that complaints from the public of poor train services are not new as, around the turn of the century, the *Peebles-shire and South Midlothian Advertiser* carried many such articles. In May 1892, Loanhead Town Council, after representation from the townspeople, complained that the frequency of trains was inadequate, and that a late service from Edinburgh on Saturdays would be popular. In his reply, John Conacher, the NBR General Manager, regretted that extra trains could not be added. His suggestion that the service from Polton be used instead brought the observation from Baillie Brown that 'if Mr Conacher had ever walked the road from Polton to Loanhead, he would never have written it'. (Polton is situated at the foot of Polton Brae, a very steep hill leading from Loanhead.) As to the additional Saturday train, if it would pay, the company would 'put one on'. Provost Young moved to accept the late train, which appeared in the timetables from then on, leaving Edinburgh at 10.55 pm or thereabouts.

Some four years later, an alteration to the Saturday afternoon service, made to suit members of the recently opened Glencorse Golf Club, came under fire from the rest of the public and the NBR was reminded in the *Advertiser* that 'there is more than one class to cater for.' The same edition also announced that a horse-drawn brake was now running between Penicuik Post Office and Glencorse station, in connection with all trains.

Over the next few years, the suggestion that the line be extended to Penicuik appears regularly. The NBR, not surprisingly, paid no heed as, apart from the cost, any extension would have affected traffic figures on its Penicuik branch.

In the early part of 1897, the employees of the Shotts Iron Co. at Straiton petitioned for a platform for their use at the junction, to avoid the walk from Loanhead and Gilmerton. In their estimate dated 10th September, the NBR stated that a wooden platform 6 ft wide could be provided at a cost of £140, which appears to have been beyond the SIC's budget, as there is no record of the platform being built.

The transfer was announced in May 1905 of the Glencorse station master, James Scott, to Broomieknoweon the Polton branch. He had started his employment on the NBR at Hassendean in the 1860s, moved to Selkirk in 1873, and was appointed station master on the opening of the Glencorse extension. Having suffered a serious illness some years previously, the NBR management had decided that the duties at Broomieknowe, a passenger-only station, would be more suited to him. His contribution to the running of the station at Glencorse, particularly the military traffic, over the 28 years was duly acknowledged in the local press.

ROSLIN and GLENCORSE BRANCH.

Notes

† No. 3.—Shunts Traffic at Millerhill. Calls at Gilmerton with Road Van Goods only.

No. 4.—Works Ramsay and Burghlee Pits as required; performs necessary shunting at Loanhead and Millerhill. Engine runs to Roslin for water at suitable time. On Tuesdays makes a cross run between Roslin and Millerhill, when required, for Live Stock. Agents, Roslin and Gilmerton, to advise Loanhead when there is Live Stock the night previous.

‡ No. 5.—Detaches Polton Carriages at Millerhill.

No. 9.—Runs combined with Penicuik train to Millerhill.

No. 10.—Works Roslin Colliery, near Roslin.

Edgefield and Standard Sidings.—Station-Master, Loanhead, must arrange for the working of Edgefield and Standard Sidings as required.

No. 2.—If through load can be got from Burghlee or Millerhill for Niddrie West, South Leith, or Granton, train may be run forward to these points instead of to Portobello.

No. 6.—Works Roslin Colliery. Performs necessary shunting at Loanhead Station and Ramsay Pit Sidings. † Calls at Gilmerton when required to leave Road Van Goods.

No. 7.—Runs combined with Dalkeith train from Millerhill to Edinburgh.

No. 8.—Performs necessary shunting at Gilmerton. Runs forward to North Leith, Granton, or South Leith if required.

No. 16.—Runs forward to Niddrie West when required, returning immediately to Millerhill.

No. 17.—Tickets to be collected at Waverley.

No. 21.—Works Roslin Colliery. Lifts only perishable traffic at Gilmerton. Gilmerton to advise Loanhead when it is necessary to do so.

WEEK-DAYS. UP TRAINS.

Stations and Sidings.	Distance from Edinburgh (M C)	1 Min.	2 Min.	3 Min.	4 Mth.	5 Pass.	6 Min.	7 Pass.	8 Pass.	9 Pass.	10 Min.	11 Pass.	12 Pass.	13 Pass.	14 Pass.	15 Pass.	16 Pass.	17 Min.	18 Pass.	19 Min.	20 Pass.
		a.m.	a.m.	a.m.	a.m.	a.m.	a.m.	a.m.	SO p.m.	SO p.m.	p.m.		SO p.m.	p.m.	p.m.	p.m.		p.m.	p.m.	S p.m.	SO p.m.
Edinburgh (Wav.) dep.				Suspended					1 30	1 30			2 55	2 30	4 57				8 52		11 20
Abbeyhill ,,									1 33	1 33			2 58	2 34	5 0				8 55		11 30
Piershill ,,	3 0								1 38	1 38			3 6	2 39	5 8						11 31
Portobello ,,	3 8								1 41	1 41	12 53		3 12	2 40	5 7			9 0	9 0	10 27	11 39
Niddrie South Junc. arr.	4 38			6 30					1 46	1 44	1 5		3 18	2 45	5 14	6 39		9 3	9 3	10 45	11 45
Do. dep.		3 25	5 40	6 35		9 50			1 53	1 48	1 58		3 21	2 50	5 22	6 47		9 9	9 7	11 11	11 46
Millerhill Jo. dep.	6 19	3 25	5 7	6 40	8 30	9 54			1 58	1 58			3 26	2 51	5 27	6 52		9 15	9 15	11 36	11 51
Gilmerton ,,	6 48			6 45		9 56			2 4	2 1	2 15		3 27	2 54	5 28	6 53		9 20		11 43	11 55
Straiton Siding ,,	8 57					10 4			2 6	2 2	2 44		3 32	3 6	5 33	6 58		8 59	9 26		11 59
Edgefield Siding ,,	9 57	3 55	6 57						2 10	2 7	2 52		3 34	3 9	5 35	7 0		9 0	Stop.	Stop.	
Loanhead arr.	10 39	3 55	6 57	8 5	8 50	10 10				2 9	2 57		3 38		5 39	7 4		9 59	9 28		
Do. dep.	10 73	4 1	6 15	8 5	Stop.	10 15				2 18	3 15								9 32		
Burghlee Siding ,,	12 12	4 8	6 20	8 10		10 17			2 4		3 20										
Roslin arr.	12 12	Stop.	8 10	Stop.		10 21															
Do. dep.																					
Glencorse arr.	14 18																				

WEEK-DAYS. DOWN TRAINS.

Stations and Sidings.	Distance from Edinburgh (M C)	1 Min.	2 Min.	3 Min.	4 Pass.	5 Pass.	6 Min.	7 Pass.	8 Min.	9 Pass.	10 Min.	11	12 Pass.	13 Pass.	14 Pass.	15 Min.	16 Pass.	17 Pass.	18 Pass.	19 Pass.	20 Pass.	21 Min.
		a.m.	a.m.	a.m.	a.m.	a.m.	a.m.	a.m.	p.m.	SO p.m.			SO p.m.	p.m.	p.m.	p.m.	SO p.m.	p.m.	p.m.	p.m.	p.m.	SO p.m.
Glencorse dep.					8 9		10 16	11 10	12 2					2 30		3 45	4 30			7 30	8 7	10 10
Roslin arr.	1 55	5 10			8 13		10 25	11 14	12 10					2 34		3 50	4 34		6 8	7 34	9 51	10 15
Do. dep.		5 10	7 10		8 14		10 30	11 15	12 25	1 58				2 39		4 0	4 35		6 13	7 35	9 55	10 30
Burghlee Siding ,,	2 22	5 37			8 18		10 35	11 19	12 38	1 59				2 40		4 20	4 39		6 17	7 39	9 56	10 38
Loanhead arr.		5 37	7 30		8 19		10 45	11 20	12 58	2 4				2 45		4 25	4 40		6 18	7 45	10 0	10 55
Do. dep.		6 30		Stop.	8 24		11 0	11 25	11 3	2 6				2 50		5 28	4 45		6 27	7 51	10 6	11 15
Straiton Siding ,,					8 29		Suspended	11 30	1 8	2 10				2 51		5 36	4 50		6 28	7 54	10 10	11 30
Gilmerton ,,					8 30			11 38						2 54		5 55	4 51			7 59	10 12	Stop.
Millerhill Jo. arr.					8 33		Gore-bridge	11 30								6 10	4 54			8 0	10 15	
Do. dep.					8 38			11 37								Stop.	4 58				10 20	
Niddrie South Junc. arr.					8 44			11 50									5 4				10 26	
Portobello ,,								11 53													Stop.	
Edinburgh (Wav.) arr.		6 45																				

Glencorse branch Working Timetable, October 1916.

World War I and the Grouping

It is often said that the period up to the start of World War I in 1914 was the 'golden age' of railways in Britain and one of the ways in which this was demonstrated was by the frequent references to the numbers of passengers reported in the local newspapers of the time. The lack of a late train back to Edinburgh on the local Monday holiday in April 1914 was criticised, as 'many intending passengers were disappointed'. The figures for Saturday 6th June, 1914 were typical of the period, with parties from the Gunpowder Works, Carpet Factory and Sunday School all leaving Roslin for various destinations, and an influx of 750 visitors arriving from Sunday schools and other organisations for the day.

It is a portent of the future to read, in another edition, that a Mr Munro of Auchindinny had started a motor bus service from Roslin to Edinburgh on the 10th July, 1914. This service does not appear to have lasted very long, presumably due to the outbreak of the war, but it is clear that the motor bus was beginning to pose a threat to train services on the branch.

At the outbreak of the war in August 1914, all railways in Britain came under Government control, and there was an increase in military traffic to and from Glencorse Barracks. As the war progressed, and more and more men were called to arms, certain stations throughout the country were closed to passengers as an economy measure. Gilmerton was amongst those chosen on the NBR, services being withdrawn from 1st January, 1917. Luckily it did not suffer the fate of some stations, which were never re-opened, and trains were restored from 2nd June, 1919, some six months after the Armistice.

In 1921 the SIC put forward a proposal for a coal screening plant to be sited immediately north of Roslin. This would have stretched for over a mile from a junction with the branch at underbridge No.15 to a point behind Manse Road, and would have resulted in a considerable increase in train movements, dealing with traffic from Roslin, Burghlee and Ramsey pits. In the event, nothing came of the scheme, but the construction of the large concrete coal washer at the Ramsey pit in 1928 appears to have dealt with the problem.

The part played by the railways during the war had been immense, but peace found them suffering from lack of investment and maintenance. Therefore, Government control continued until 1921, when proposals were put forward to group the 120 or so main railway companies into four, the North British to be included in the London and North Eastern Railway group. This took effect from 1st January, 1923.

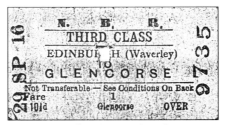

NBR ticket issued for a journey on the Glencorse branch in 1916.   *Andrew Bethune*

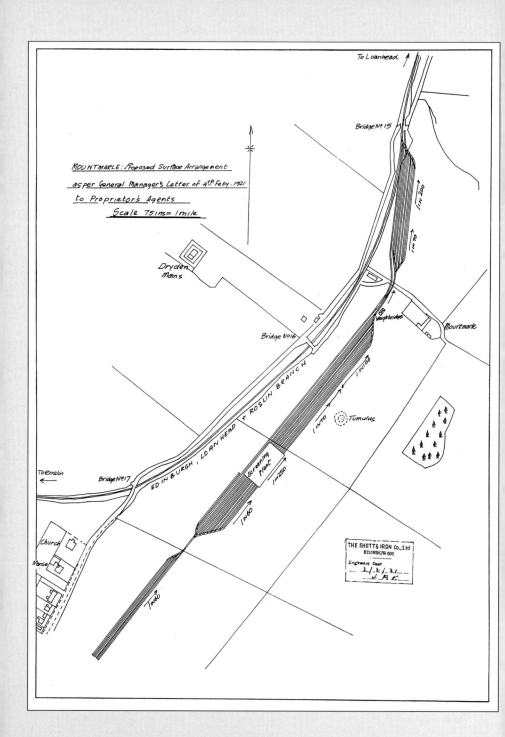

MOUNTMARLE: Proposed Surface Arrangement
as per General Manager's Letter of 4th Feby. 1921
to Proprietor's Agents
Scale 75ins = 1 mile

To Loanhead

Bridge No. 15

1 in 200

1 in 70

Dryden Mains

Weighbridge

Mountmarle

Bridge No. 16

ROSLIN BRANCH

1 in 60

1 in 60

Tumulus

EDINBURGH, LOAN HEAD

To Roslin

Bridge No. 17

Screening Plant

1 in 250

1 in 60

1 in 60

Church

Manse

THE SHOTTS IRON Co., Ltd
EDINBURGH.
Engineers Dept
2/.2/.21
J.B.K.

Chapter Six

Grouping and Closure to Passengers

Apart from the name of the new company appearing on official documents and uniforms, the branch carried on in much the same manner that it had always done. Even the regular branch locomotive at the time remained in NBR livery for some years, and no improvements were apparent in passenger rolling stock.

The addition of a large coal washing plant at the Ramsey Colliery in 1928 led to an increase in transfer traffic from both Roslin and Burghlee, as well as adding a local landmark, visible for miles around. More importantly for the miners, pithead baths were also provided.

By 1930, passenger figures, which had remained steady at around half of the pre-1914 totals during the 1920s, began to decline, particularly at Glencorse. Roslin remained healthy, due mainly to the still extensive summer excursion traffic, while Gilmerton maintained its position at the bottom of the table.

For some time all four railway companies had been anxious to invest in road transport, both passenger and freight, as a means of coping with a widening world of competition. The Road Traffic Act of 1928 enabled the Big Four to achieve this aim, and they embarked on a programme of acquiring existing road transport undertakings or, at least, a substantial interest in them. Both the LNER and the LMS eventually had a 50 per cent share in the Scottish Motor Traction Co., although they were not permitted to run bus services themselves. It may have been assumed that this interest would lead to an integration of road and rail services but, in the event, the opposite happened, with a large number of branches losing their passenger services within five years, the Glencorse branch amongst them.

By the early 1930s, the Scottish Motor Traction Co. operated an extensive number of routes radiating from Edinburgh. Gilmerton was served by a staggering total of 66 buses in each direction daily, as the village lay on the Edinburgh-Dalkeith route. Loanhead was served from 5.45 am until 10.55 pm by 43 services. Both rail and bus journey times to Loanhead were identical at 24 minutes, the advantage of a more direct road being offset by lower speeds. The bus route served more of the City, however, and avoided the traditional blustery exit via the Waverley steps to Princes Street.

While Loanhead benefitted from being on both the Penicuik and Lasswade routes, giving an average 20 minute headway, Roslin and Glencorse passengers could make use of the hourly service to Penicuik. In addition, Glencorse could be reached by using the Penicuik via Lothianburn and the hourly Peebles services. In the other direction, Glencorse, Roslin and Loanhead were connected by the Penicuik-Dalkeith route, which made frequent connections with the Edinburgh-Polton Mill services at Loanhead.

'G8' class 0-4-4T No. 354 accelerates a Glencorse train on the main line near Portobello. Note the immaculate condition of the locomotive and the spartan passenger stock in use.   *H.L. Salmon*

The crew of class 'M' 4-4-2T No. 53 take a break at Glencorse in NBR days. Nicknamed 'Yorkies' from their having been built by the Yorkshire Engine Co., No. 53 was built in 1913, lasting into British Railways' ownership until 1952.   *Kenneth Williamson*

Class 'P' 0-4-4T No. 1327 pauses at Millerhill with a branch train in 1924. Classified 'G8' by the LNER, it was withdrawn in May 1925, without being renumbered. *R.W. Lynn Collection*

Guard Hutchinson takes pride of place in front of class 'M' 0-4-4T No. 354 at Roslin in 1925, while driver McArthur looks on from the footplate. Some two years after the Grouping, No. 354 still carries NBR livery, and lasted until September 1936. *G.N. Heathcote Collection*

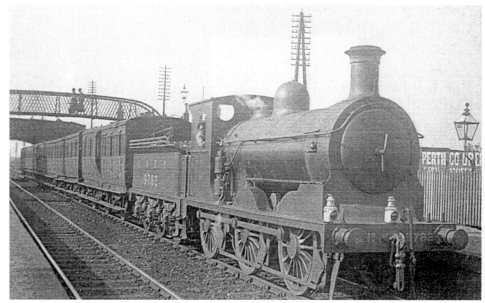

While primarily goods locomotives, those class 'C' ('J36') 0-6-0s which were fitted with the Westinghouse brake were used on passenger services, as illustrated by No. 9782 at Millerhill in June 1925 with a branch train. *J.T. Rutherford*

Ex-NBR brake third No. 31145 appears none the worst for its involvement as the first coach behind the engine in the fatal derailment of 1912. *A.G. Dunbar, courtesy A.A. McLean*

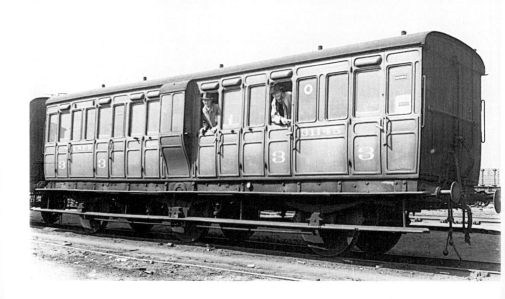

1st May 1932

GLENCORSE BRANCH.

WEEK-DAYS.

UP TRAINS. Stations and Sidings.	Distance from Edinburgh	1 Min.	2 Min.	3‡ Pass.	4 Min.	5 Min.	6 Min.	7 Pass.	8 Pass.	9 Pass.	10 Pass.	11 Pass.	11a	12 Pass.
Departs from ... {		Burgh lee 6a40		...	...	...	...	...	...	...	...	...	ͻ	...
	Miles Chns	a.m.	a.m.	a.m.	SX a.m.	SX p.m.	SO p.m.	SO p.m.	SO p.m.	p.m.	p.m.	SO p.m.		SO p.m.
Edinburgh (Wav.) ...dep.	... ...	...	...	...	9 41	...	...	1 31	3 10	5 6	...	9 3	...	11 0
Abbeyhill ... ... ,,	... ...	...	...	......	9 44	......	......	1 34	3 13	......	......	......		......
Piershill ... ... ,,	... ...	...	...	...	...	......	...	1 37	3 16	5 10	....	......		......
Portobello ... ,,	3 0	...	...	......	9 49	10 39	12§30	12 35	1 40	3 19	5 13	......	9 9	......	11 6
Niddrie South Junction ,,	4 33	...	...	...	9 52	10 46	12 38	12 42	1 43	3 22	...	...	9 12		11 9
Millerhill Junction ... arr.	6 19	...	...	......	...	12 47	12 50	......	...	...	...	...		...
—	Millerhill Junc. ...dep.	... ...	5 0	8 45	9 55	10 53	1 55	2 0	1 46	3 25	5 19	6 46	9 15	...	11 12
Gilmerton ... ,,	8 43	......	9 10	10 1	......	......	......	1 52	3 31	5 25	6 52	...		...
Straiton Siding ... ,,	9 57	...	...	...	...	...	...	...	...	...	...	...		...
•	Edgefield Siding ... ,,	9 78	...	...	...	...	...	...	...	...	...	...	...		...
Loanhead ... { arr.	10 39	5 25	9 25	10 5	...	2‡14	2 19	1 56	3 35	5 29	6 56	9 23	...	11 20
—	Loanhead ... { dep.	... ...	5 35	......	10 8	11 18	......	2 55	1 57	3 36	5 30	6 57	9 24	......	11 21
	Burghlee Siding ... ,,	10 73	5 40	...	...	...	......	...	...	...	...	...	...		...
—	Roslin ... { arr.	12 12	......	......	10 12	......	......	3 3	...	...	...	...	...		...
	Roslin ... { dep.	... ...	......	......	10 15	11 33	...	3 20	2 2	3 41	5 35	7 2	9 29	......	11 26
	Roslin Colliery ... arr.	12 35	...	...	......	11 38	...	...	...	...	...	...	...		...
—	Glencorse ... ,,	14 13	......	...	10 19	...	....	3 30	2 6	3 45	5 39	7 6	9 33	...	11 30

WEEK-DAYS.

DOWN TRAINS. Stations and Sidings.	Distance from Glencorse	13 Min.	13a Pass.	14 Pass.	15 Min.	16 Pass.	17 Min.	18 Pass.	19 Pass.	20 Min.	21 Min.	22 Pass.	23 Pass.	24 Pass.
Departs from ... {		Miller hill 5 a 0	Co'mences Junc.	May only.	Miller hill 8a45	...	...	...	...	Porto bello 12p35	Porto bello Yard 12p30	...	...	...
	Miles Chns	a.m.	a.m.	a.m.	a.m.	SO p.m.	SX p.m.	SO p.m.	p.m.	SO p.m.	SX p.m.	p.m.	SO p.m.	SO p.m.
—	Glencorse ...dep.	... ...	...	7 51	8 3	...	12 38	...	2 18	3 59	4 10	...	6 21	7 41	10 2
	Roslin Colliery ... ,,	1 58	...	...	...	...	...	2 5	...	...	...	...	...	...	...
—	Roslin ... { arr.	2 1	...	...	...	...	...	...	...	...	4 15	...	...	...	...
	Roslin ... { dep.	... ...	...	7 55	8 7	...	12 42	2 15	2 22	4 3	4 20	......	6 25	7 45	10 6
	Burghlee Siding ... ,,	3 20	6 40	...	...	...	...	...	...	...	4 30	...	...	...	...
—	Loanhead ... { arr.	3 54	...	7 59	8 11	...	12 46	...	2 26	4 7	4 35	...	6 29	7 49	10 10
—	Loanhead ... { dep.	... ...	6 50	8 0	8 12	11 20	12 47	2 55	2 27	4 8	5 35	5 35	6 30	7 50	10 11
	Straiton Siding ... ,,	4 36	......	...	...	......	...	...	...	...	5 46	5 46	......	......	......
	Gilmerton ... ,,	5 50	...	8 4	8 16	...	12 51	...	2 31	4 12	6 2	6 2	6 34	...	...
—	Millerhill Junc. ... arr.	7 74	7 20	8 8	8 20	11 58	12 55	3 20	2 35	4 16	6 22	6 22	6 38	7 57	10 18
	Millerhill Junction ...dep.	... ...	......	8 9	8 21	...	12 56	...	2 36	4 17	7 27	7 27	...	7 58	10 19
	Niddrie South Junction ,,	9 60	......	8 12	8 24	...	12 59	...	2 39	4 20	7 33	7 33	...	8 1	10 22
	Portobello ... ,,	11 13	......	8 15	8 27	...	1 2	...	2 42	4 23	7 54	7 54	...	8 4	10 25
	Piershill ... ,,		...	...	8 30	...	...	...	......	4 26	...	...	...	...	...
	Abbeyhill ... ,,		...	...	...	...	‡	...	2 47	4 29	...	...	...	...	...
	Edinburgh (Wav.) ... arr.	14 13	...	8 21	8 35	...	1 8	...	2 50	4 32	...	...	...	8 10	10 31
Arrives at ... {		Loan head 9 25		...	...	...	...	...	...	...	...	...	...	...	...

No. 2.—Conveys Edinburgh and Glencorse Road Van (which must be a braked vehicle) to Loanhead to be taken forward to Glencorse by 9.41 a.m. Passenger train *ex* Edinburgh.

No. 3.—‡ Conveys Edinburgh and Glencorse Road Van from Loanhead to Glencorse.

No. 4.—On Saturdays only engine and trainmen work 10.20 a.m., Niddrie West to Tweedmouth and back.

No. 5.—§ Portobello Yard. ‡ After arrival at Loanhead will perform necessary shunting there, also at Straiton, Standard and Edgefield Sidings, making trip to Burghlee Colliery, if necessary.

No. 6.—Works Roslin Colliery, near Roslin.

No. 13.—Load to be restricted to 30 wagons Mineral from Loanhead to Millerhill, or as instructed by Southern Control Office.

No. 15.—Works all Sidings at Loanhead, Ramsay, Straiton and Gilmerton. Engine proceeds from Millerhill to Portobello to take up the working of the 12.30 p.m. S X, Portobello Yard to Loanhead (12.35 p.m. S O, Portobello to Glencorse).

No. 16.—† Crosses to North Line at Abbeyhill Junction.

No. 17.—After arrival at Millerhill makes trip to Portobello or Niddrie West as instructed by Control Office.

Edgefield and Standard Sidings.—Station Master, Loanhead, must arrange for the working of Edgefield and Standard Sidings as required.

Glencorse Branch Passenger Engine and Guard.—On arrival at Glencorse at 10.19 a.m., will make Goods trip to Eastfield Siding (which is a Daylight Siding) and back about 11.0 a.m. daily. Except on Saturdays, it will thereafter proceed to Loanhead, lifting traffic from Roslin and performing any necessary shunting at these places.

Glencorse branch Working Timetable, 1st May, 1932.

The Axe Falls

As reported by the *Peeblesshire and South Midlothian Advertiser's* 'Special Representative', in the edition of 21st April, 1933, notices had been posted at the stations on the branch to the effect that passenger services would cease as from 1st May. The article then proceeded to give a short history of the branch (mostly inaccurate). In fact, the LNER had been considering the implications of the withdrawal of passenger services for some time, and had drawn up a plan, dated 9th June, 1930, showing proposed simplification of the signalling arrangements at Roslin and Glencorse. The accompanying report, dated 16th March, 1933, appears to be correct in stating that 'it is not anticipated that any serious complaints will arise from the public', as the closure was not even discussed in the local newspapers. The passenger receipts for the year ending 30th June, 1932 are given as £256, while the cost of running the service was £1,612. A net saving of £2,566 is also quoted, as a result of discontinuing the service and closing the signal boxes at Gilmerton, Roslin and Glencorse.

The 'Special Representative' also travelled on the last train, the 11.00 pm (Saturdays only) from Waverley, and reported:

> Very little public interest was evinced in the closing of Glencorse branch railway line on Saturday night, probably due to the inclement weather. Only a few passengers bound for Roslin joined the train at Loanhead, and it is doubtful whether they gave more than a passing thought to the fact that it was the last occasion they would be able to make that journey. There was certainly no flag waving and no demonstration of any kind, and so the last train passed.

A charabanc party at Mrs Young's Roslin tea rooms, in the 1920s. The railway could do little to compete with this type of excursion traffic, which contributed to the demise of the passenger service.   *George Campbell*

Chapter Seven

A Quiet Backwater
1933-1961

The swiftness of the withdrawal of the passenger service had obviously taken the local population by surprise and, although there had been little evidence of protest before 1st May, it was not long before the subject was raised by Loanhead Town Council. It had been observed that the LNER was continuing to run the customary special excursions for local organisations, Loanhead West Church Sunday School, for example, sending 500 children and adults to Burntisland on 10th June, 1933. At the Council meeting held on the Monday following closure, the suggestion was made that the service be reinstated on Saturdays only, as the public were finding it very difficult to reach Portobello, which was still the favourite local destination for a 'day at the seaside'. The alternative of asking the Scottish Motor Traction Co. (SMT) to start a through Saturday service to Portobello was also put forward. The Town Clerk was instructed to contact both companies on the subject but, not unsurprisingly, a negative reply was received from the LNER and none at all recorded from the SMT.

Having rid itself of the burden of running a passenger service, the LNER could now concentrate on transporting the output from the four remaining collieries (Roslin, Burghlee, Ramsey and Gilmerton). While the northern part of the branch remained busy, the Glencorse extension became something of a 'withered arm', looked on by train crews as an easy run in the country.

The goods service was altered slightly, with an additional train timed to start from Millerhill Junction at 4.53 pm, taking advantage of the lack of afternoon traffic. The first goods train from Portobello now also included the parcels traffic formerly carried by passenger train.

Improvements at Loanhead

By the 1930s, Mactaggart, Scott at Loanhead were producing seaplane catapults which were mounted on Royal Navy battleships. Powered by a cordite charge, which launched the aircraft at up to 63 mph from rest, the finished structure measured 46 feet long in the stowed position. Before 1937, when the connection was provided from the goods yard to the works, it was common practice after final testing in the assembly shop to dismantle each catapult and transport it in sections by road to the goods yard. Here it was re-assembled on a bogie bolster wagon, with a match truck at either end, to cope with the excessive overhang.

Presumably the worsening situation in Europe influenced the decision to provide the company with siding accommodation, as the majority of the company's output up to this point had not been delivered by rail. The connection was made from a new siding for Veitch, the local coal merchant, which was built adjacent to the east boundary of the goods yard.

A postcard view of Loanhead, showing the contrast in building style of the 1894 extension, with its canopy. The photograph was taken from the Ramsey Colliery sidings, and the loop can be seen in the foreground.   *Alan Maclaren*

Loanhead station, with the recently opened school in the left background. Some of the station staff have congregated in the yard for the photograph, which appears to have been taken from the Ramsey washer. The colliery sidings are well filled, and a horse-drawn cart can just be seen on the weighbridge.   *Alan Maclaren*

There are no signs of life in this bleak view of Roslin, thought to be taken sometime in the 1930s, as the nameboard is still in place.   *Lens of Sutton*

The ivy-covered station building at Gilmerton, seen in the mid-1930s, with a dog as the sole occupant of the platform.   *Professor Fordyce*

The remains of Roslin engine shed, seen on 19th June, 1936. The water tank, once the subject of much discussion during the first years of the line, remains to supply the water crane on the platform. *Professor Fordyce*

Typifying the excursions run after the withdrawal of passenger services, 'J35' class 0-6-0 No. 9850 waits for the guard's whistle at Loanhead with what appears to be a Sunday School special. *J.L. Stevenson*

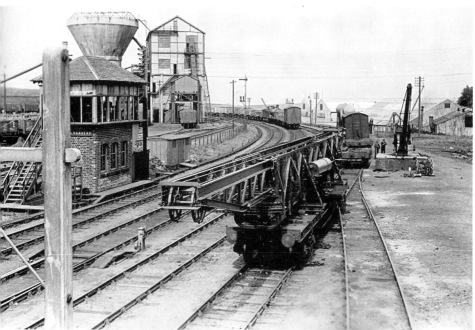

While the cordite catapult on the bogie bolster wagon was the main subject of this photograph, with the passage of time the background has become even more interesting. Taken around 1933, it shows the signal box and the Ramsey washer on the left, and an ex-NBR 0-6-0 waiting patiently in the background for the photographer to finish. In the group gathered round the yard crane, one railwayman has decided on a spot of sunbathing in the barrow, to the amusement of his workmates. *MacTaggart, Scott & Co. Ltd*

A side view of the MacTaggart, Scott catapult, in the retracted position and ready to be chained down to the 'Quint' bogie bolster wagon. Thought to be an ex-North Eastern Railway vehicle, it may have originally been built for the War Department. *MacTaggart, Scott & Co. Ltd*

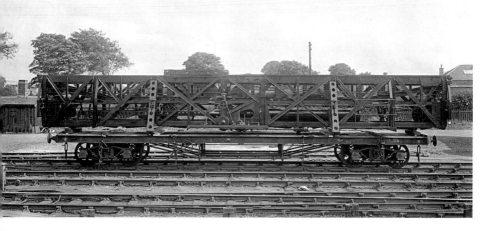

An aerial view of Loanhead, looking east. The branch can be traced running from upper left to lower right, with the Ramsey Colliery and the station in the centre. The date is sometime in 1939, as the Town Council estate in Hunter Avenue (visible above the station) is under construction. Note the colliery explosives store in isolation to the left of the main pit buildings.

MacTaggart, Scott & Co. Ltd

Three photographs taken during the clearance tests of the new private sidings at MacTaggart, Scott, in 1937, utilising an unidentified 'J35' locomotive. *Top:* The locomotive is descending the 1 in 22 gradient from the goods yard, observed by a bricklayer. Note the high level shunt signal on the embankment. *Centre:* Looking north at the newly-built heavy fitting shop, with the 'J35' at the limit of engine working. The warning notice on the sliding doors is still preserved *in situ* in 1999. *Bottom:* The 'gaffer' in his bowler hat, directing operations. *(All) MacTaggart, Scott & Co. Ltd*

A view to the west, with the Pentland hills in the background. Loanhead is on the left, with the branch running across the photograph, passing Edgefield farm on the extreme right. The shale bing at Straiton is in the middle distance.

MacTaggart, Scott & Co. Ltd

With the outbreak of World War II, troop trains made their appearance once again, with double-heading in some cases. During the war years, only one train appeared in the Working Timetable, as the output from the collieries was dealt with on an 'as required' basis by Control. The cessation of hostilities in 1945 did not result in a reduction of military traffic, as Glencorse Depot was used as a military hospital and re-habilitation centre for a number of years.

The 1st January, 1947 saw the first result of the Labour Government's nationalisation programme, with the formation of the National Coal Board (NCB). Under the NCB, all four collieries became part of Scottish Division, Area No. 2, (but not the Straiton limeworks, which was sold, as explained in Appendix Two). This resulted in the gradual disappearance of the private owner wagon, which had been a feature of goods trains since the last century. They were retained by the NCB for internal use at collieries, being gradually replaced by all-steel vehicles as the restrictions on the use of steel were eased.

Exactly one year later, the four railway companies were also nationalised, and the branch became part of British Railways (Scottish Region). As in 1923, little change was to be seen for some years; coal remained the main source of fuel in the country, and branches such as Glencorse were vital in transporting the output from collieries.

On 25th April, 1951 the branch was traversed by one of the earliest special trains organised for railway enthusiasts. Drawn by ex-NBR 'Glen' class 4-4-0 locomotive No. 62471 *Glen Falloch*, it also visited Kirkliston and South Queensferry.

Although the full potential of the branch may not have been realised up to that time, the commencment of the sinking of a mineshaft at a site in Bilston Glen to the south-west of Burghlee Colliery in 1952 was to give the line a new lease of life. The new colliery would not open until the next decade, simply due to the then limits of mining technology.

In 1955, British Railways published its Modernisation Plan. All areas of the railway operation had been reviewed and decisions made as to the way forward, within the perceived wisdom of the time. Ever since the railways had started to carry freight, wagons had been collected and sorted in marshalling yards, which had originally been built to suit each railway company's needs. This had resulted in a large number of small and medium sized yards scattered throughout the country, Edinburgh being no exception. Part of the Plan called for new 'hump' marshalling yards, where wagons are shunted up a short steep ramp (or hump), and sorted by gravity, running into a fan of sidings. All movements are controlled from one control room, which operates the points remotely and works to a prepared plan. The area immediately to the north of Millerhill station was chosen as the site of just such a yard to be known as 'Millerhill New Yard' for the Edinburgh area, with 100 sorting sidings and the capacity to deal with 5,000 wagons per day.

This is the only known photograph of Gilmerton signal box, albeit after closure. It also shows, from left to right, Station Road, the station master's house with the colliery manager's house behind, the original pithead gear and the bridge over the line to the second shaft, added in 1928. The remains of the original connection to the first shaft can be seen running behind the signal box.   *Lens of Sutton*

No. 62471 draws up at the platform at Glencorse, showing the demolished central section of the station building, on 25th April, 1951.   *Ron Glendinning*

No. 62471 *Glen Falloch* brings the 1951 special through the 'tunnel', up the 1 in 70 to Glencorse station. Glencorse School can be seen above the locomotive. *Ron Glendinning*

In May 1955, an unidentified 'J35' class 0-6-0, with guard Jock Hill at the ready, drifts towards Millerhill Junction with a train off the branch. Note the down sidings on the left, and the NBR signals, including the tall branch down home, sited on the right hand side of the cutting. This scene was to change completely in the next few years, with the construction of the hump marshalling yard. *Rae Montgomery*

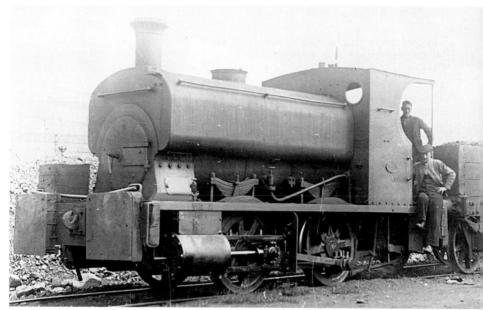

An early view of Shotts Iron Co. No. 6, at Ramsey Colliery. This locomotive is thought to have been built at Shotts *c*. 1909.
F. Jones

No. 6 was renumbered 14 by the NCB, and pauses in the sun in 1952, complete with wooden tender.
F. Jones

Closure of the Extension

In common with many other lines in Britain at this time, branch traffic was falling to unacceptable levels, with the exception of that dealt with at Loanhead. The closure of Penicuik gasworks, in 1956, when the town was connected to a new main from Edinburgh, had removed the last regular traffic from the extension. The line was cut back shortly thereafter, to a point south of Glencorse station, providing a headshunt to deal with troop trains. Accordingly, freight services were withdrawn from Gilmerton, Roslin and Glencorse from Monday 31st August, 1959 and the branch was closed beyond Roslin Colliery when a buffer stop was erected 250 yds beyond the connection to the colliery, forming a headshunt. The loop at Roslin was retained, worked from a 5-lever ground frame. In the goods yard the two sidings left after the loading bank siding had been removed in February 1957 were also retained, with their ground frame.

Even as late as the summer of 1960, passenger excursions were to be found, with the East Church Sunday School outing to North Berwick on Saturday 4th June. 300 adults and a similar number of children filled eight coaches, leaving Loanhead at 10.05 am and returning after eight hours at the popular East Lothian resort. The train was subject to a 20 mph speed restriction on the branch.

Such was the pace of railway closures at this period, that it was the summer of 1961 before the station sidings and ground frame at Gilmerton were lifted, leaving only the connection to the colliery. This minor alteration was soon overshadowed by the comprehensive changes undertaken to deal with the increase in coal traffic from Bilston Glen Colliery and the completion of Millerhill New Yard, which are dealt with in the next chapter.

This shot of Gilmerton is the only one to show the loading bank and crane, which was still *in situ* on 17th April, 1955.   *J.L. Stevenson*

The empty stock of the military special leaves Millerhill Junction for Glencorse on Saturday 4th July, 1959. With a load of at least ten coaches, 'J37' No. 64577 and 'J38' No. 65915 make an impressive sight as they attack the 1 in 55 gradient. The train would be too long for the loop, resulting in some complicated shunting at the terminus.   *Rae Montgomery*

David Ewart (*third from right*) and other members of the band of the Royal Scots Territorials march past Penicuik Gas Works on their way to Glencorse station, on the same day. They would there board the military special for their summer camp, at Sennybridge, South Wales.

David Ewart

Chapter Eight

A New Era
1961-1989

The start of a new decade saw the beginning of a new prosperity for the line, tempered by the loss of some long-standing sources of traffic. Bilston Glen Colliery opened in April 1961, after many years of development, as one of the National Coal Board's showpiece collieries. The two shafts, No. 1 at 505 feet deep and No. 2 at 510 feet had taken nine years to complete. The twin coal washers, wagon traversers and extensive array of sidings made an impressive sight for local residents, and the modern above ground facilities were much appreciated by the miners, when compared with other pits in the area.

At the time of opening, the single diesel shunter, which had been at work assisting the contractor since it had been delivered in 1959, was joined by two others, all 0-4-0s supplied by Messrs Andrew Barclay, Sons & Co. Ltd, Kilmarnock. Unusually, all were supplied with 4-wheel brake tenders, to assist in the handling of the large rakes of wagons which were envisaged.

However, two sources of traffic were lost in 1961, namely Straiton Sidings and Gilmerton Colliery. Production at the once thriving workings at Straiton had been declining steadily, with the reduction in the use of limestone in general and, being a privately owned concern, had reached the point where it had become uneconomic. Fuller details are given in Appendix Two.

Gilmerton Colliery suffered a disastrous fire which led to its premature closure, with the miners being found jobs in other pits in the area. Again, the pit buildings and sidings were left *in situ*.

To assist in working the increased Bilston Glen traffic, the track layout at Loanhead was altered, as described in Chapter Twelve. These alterations were brought into use on Monday 11th September, 1961.

Millerhill Yard opens

Constructed at a cost of £3,000,000, the new yard was brought into use in June 1962, straddling the Edinburgh-Carlisle main line, between Millerhill Junction and Newcraighall. The up platform edge of Millerhill station, closed to passengers traffic on 7th November, 1955, had been cut back, leaving the station building and house intact, but the remainder of the site, including the down platform and the former branch bay, was completely cleared as part of the alterartions to accommodate the new track layout. A replacement concrete overbridge, twice as wide as the original, to span the new down yard arrival sidings, was also necessary. On the approach from the branch itself, a new loop line diverged just north of the A6106 overbridge, with a sand drag to intercept runaways. Two sidings were provided next to the foundry, from the connection to the newly opened Monktonhall Colliery.

Millerhill Junction signal box was replaced, along with two other local boxes (Niddrie South Junction and Glenesk Junction) by a single modern box situated

The extensive sidings at Bilston Glen are pictured soon after opening in 1961. The viewpoint is from the footbridge which carried a public footpath over the new sidings.   *Author's Collection*

One of the wagon traversers at Bilston Glen, powered by MacTaggart, Scott hydraulics, is the subject of this photograph which was taken shortly after the opening of the colliery.
MacTaggart, Scott & Co. Ltd

In addition to the new surface locomotives at Bilston Glen, three narrow gauge battery locomotives were provided. The second of these is seen at the Stockton-on-Tees works of Metrovick-Beyer, Peacock, with two of the short-lived D5700 series Co-Bo diesels for British Railways under construction in the background. *R.A. Darville*

The Andrew Barclay works photograph of No. 451, one of the shunters supplied in 1959 to the Lady Victoria Colliery, and later transferred to Bilston Glen. It was supplied with a small brake tender, as shown. *Hunslet Barclay Ltd, with the permission of the Keeper of the Records of Scotland*

The passenger entrance of Loanhead station in 1964, with the Ramsey Colliery in the background.   *Author*

The Loanhead station building, pictured on a grey Sunday afternoon in 1964, appears to be in reasonable external condition. Note that the platform has been cut short after the demolition of the wooden centre section of the original building.   *Author*

A quiet Sunday at Loanhead in 1964, with the goods yard filled with a load of concrete pipes destined for a local drainage project.   *Author*

Loanhead goods yard, in the summer of 1964, with the Ramsey 'pug' in the left background, partially hidden by the up home signal, with the miniature arm visible, controlling the exit from the loop. Veitch's coal delivery lorry is being loaded on the extreme right.   *Author*

Enginemen	6.15am. to 2.15pm.		SX.
(St. Margarets)	12.15pm. to 8.15pm.		SX
	(Engine Prepared)		
Millerhill	6.47am. to 2.47pm.		SX
Guard	12.15pm to 8.15pm		SX

S.X.

		a.m.
St. Margarets E.S.		6.30 LE
Millerhill	A	7.30
Loanhead		7.55
Bilston Glen	B	8.50
Slateford		10.10
Kingsknowe		11.10
		p.m.
Loanhead		1.20
Bilston Glen		2.10
Slateford	C	3.40 E/V.
Millerhill		5.0
Bilston Glen		6.30
Millerhill		7.45 LE
St. Margarets E.S.		8.0

Notes
A. Conveys General traffic for Branch and empty Mineral Wagons. Station traffic for Loanhead to be next to brake van.
B. Lifts full engine load - reduce at Duddingston.
C. Engine and Van to Duddingston or Millerhill for empties.
LE Light Engine

First shift to be relieved at Loanhead by Liaison Car.

Enginemen	4.55am. to 1.20pm.		SX.
(St. Margarets)	(Engine Prepared)		
Millerhill	5.32am. to 1.32pm.		SX
Guard			

		a.m.
St. Margarets E.S.		5.10 LE
Millerhill	A	6.15
Loanhead		7.15
Burghlee Colliery	B	8.0
Millerhill		9.0

Notes
A. Assists E.84 Millerhill to Loanhead

B. Uplift despatch traffic for Millerhill Down Reception
LE Light Engine

Enginemen	4.55am. to 1.25pm.		
	2.0pm. to 10.30pm.		SX.
Millerhill	5.32am to 1.32pm		
Guard	2.17pm. to 10.17pm		SX
	(Engine Prepared)		

		a.m.
St. Margarets E.S.		5.10 LE.
Millerhill	A	6.15
Loanhead	B	6.50
Roslin Colliery	C	9.5
Bilston Glen	D	9.50
Loanhead	E	10.40
Bilston Glen	F	11.50
		p.m.
Millerhill		12.55 LE
St. Margarets		1.10

Fresh engine to be supplied for second shift

S.X.

		a.m.
St. Margarets E.S.		2.15 LE
Millerhill	G	3.0
Loanhead	H	3.35
Roslin Colliery	I	4.20
Bilston Glen	J	5.40
Millerhill		7.0 E/V.
Bilston Glen		8.30
Millerhill		9.45 LE
St. Margarets E.S.		10.0

Notes
A. E.84 assist by E.86 conveys 60 M.Ws. for Roslin and Burghlee Collieries
B. Works empty M.W. to Roslin Colliery.
C. Lifts general and washer traffic, detach former at Burghlee Colliery.
D. Lifts all washer traffic for Ramsay Washer.
E. Works empty M.Ws. to Bilston Glen.
F. Lifts rough load for Millerhill.
G. E.84 assisted by E.96 conveys 60 M.Ws to Loanhead
H. Works M.Ws to Roslin Colliery when required.
I. Uplifts balance of traffic.
J. Lifts Millerhill load.
LE Light Engine

Enginemen	2.0 pm. to 10.0pm.		SX.
(St. Margarets)	(Engine Prepared)		
Millerhill Guard	2.22pm. to 10.22pm.		

SX

		p.m..
St. Margarets E.S.		2.15 LE
Millerhill	A	3.0
Loanhead		3.40
Bilston Glen		4.15
Slateford		6.0
Kingsknowe		7.0
Millerhill		8.0
Works to Control Orders		
St. Margarets E.S.		9.45

Notes
A. Assists E.84 to Loanhead
LE Light Engine

Working Timetable for April 1964.

Left: No. 65929 with the last E98 trip of the day cautiously approaches Millerhill Yard, in March 1964, the last year of steam working.
Author

Below: An unidentified 'J38' class 0-6-0, in filthy external condition, brings the afternoon E58 Bilston Glen-Slateford working through Gilmerton in August 1964. The connection to the former colliery had not been brought into use by Bernard Hunter Ltd at this period.
Author

Above: The Railway Society of Scotland railtour pauses at Loanhead on 7th October, 1967. The derelict Ramsey Colliery forms the background.   *G.N. Turnbull*

Right: In 1968, under the watchful gaze of their foreman, Adam Johnston, Tom Inglis (*standing*) and Alex Kerr sheet over a tube wagon, in the MacTaggart, Scott sidings. The load consists of a set of hydraulic deck machinery destined for the HMS *Hecla*, an Ocean Survey vessel.   *MacTaggart, Scott & Co. Ltd*

within the yard, controlling all services on the Edinburgh-Carlisle main line and trains entering and leaving the yard.

With the commissioning of Millerhill yard, the modernisation of the northern end of the branch was almost complete, and with steam power gradually being replaced by diesel in the next few years, the line appeared to have a bright future. Goods traffic continued to be dealt with at Loanhead, although parcels had been collected and delivered by railway road motor since the 1959 closure of the other branch stations.

The rationalisation at Roslin was completed on 7th January, 1963, when the two remaining station sidings were removed. By this time the site of the colliery at Gilmerton had passed into the ownership of a well-known local scrap merchant, Bernard Hunter, who was in favour of rail transport. After some reorganisation, two sidings were retained for handling this traffic.

The NCB was evidently carrying out its own rationalisation programme, as Burghlee Colliery was closed in October 1964, followed by Ramsey Colliery in December 1965, after over a century of production. The steam winding engine, which could be heard locally for a considerable distance, fell silent.

Having lain derelict since closure, the main part of the Ramsey Colliery site, including the area adjacent to the line, was bought in 1968 by another scrap dealer, Motor Spares and Salvage Ltd (later Autoparts), who had been located beside the Edinburgh-Glasgow main line at Gogar. A tall corrugated steel fence was erected around the property, including the Washer, which remained one of the local landmarks.

The opening of a new 1,200,000 kw coal fired power station on the south shore of the River Forth at Cockenzie on Friday 24th May, 1968 appeared to have secured the future of the branch for many years. Requiring up to 12,200 tonnes of coal per day, the new station was to be supplied from various collieries, including Bilston Glen, using the 'Merry-Go-Round' system. Dedicated block

To act as a standby, a Barclay 'pug' was sent to Bilston Glen, but saw little use. By September 1977, she was dumped at the end of the headshunt, missing most of the external fittings. She was originally supplied in 1934 to Fleets Colliery, Tranent.   *Bill Roberton*

Taken from the former point of divergence of the line to Roslin, this August 1982 view shows the track layout at Bilston Glen.   *Author*

The array of sidings leading to Bilston Glen make an impressive sight. The buffer stop of the cripple wagon siding is visible, *centre right*.   *Author*

Class '20' Nos. 20 204 and 20 203 double-head the standard rake of 29 hoppers towards Millerhill yard, in this view taken on 9th March, 1981.   *Bill Roberton*

The final resting place of the three original Bilston Glen shunters was a scrapyard in Inverkeithing, where Nos. 98, 32 and 10 were photographed on 30th March, 1987. The cabs had been previously removed to allow their transport by road from the colliery.   *Bill Roberton*

Latterly 350 hp class '08' shunters were hired from BR, when the NCB locomotives were
unserviceable. On this occasion No. 08 570 was in charge on 1st March, 1988.   *Dr M. Rhodes*

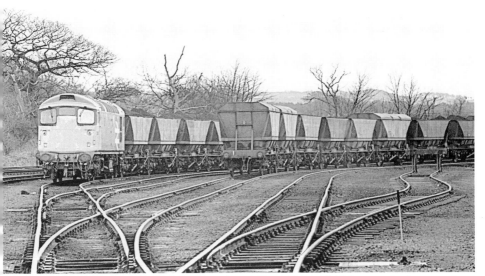

Class '26' No. 26 005 appears to be ready to leave Bilston Glen with 29 hoppers for Longannet Power Station in Fife, on 1st March, 1988. Some of the hopper wagons still have their hoods fitted at this time.   *Dr M. Rhodes*

Class '37' No. 37 675 enters the wagon unloading facility at Cockenzie Power Station at the regulation 0.5 mph. The entire train of HAA hoppers will be emptied in only a few minutes.
                                                                                    Author

trains of 32 tonne hopper wagons shuttled back and forth, hauled by locomotives fitted for slow-speed working, to maintain the 915,000 tonne stockpile.

Roslin Colliery Closes

There had been a proposal to close Roslin Colliery some years before, causing anxiety in the village, but production continued. When the NCB announced in the winter of 1968 that the colliery would close in the following January, this time there was to be no reprieve. With the loss of this traffic, the line could be abandoned from the north end of Bilston viaduct, thus offering a considerable saving in maintenance costs. However, BR did not appear to be in any hurry to remove the track, as it was not officially taken out of use until April 1972. The opportunity was also taken to rationalise the layout at Loanhead, with the closure of the goods shed and signal box. All sidings were taken up (with the exception of that serving the coal merchant), while the main line was slewed to ease the curve through the station area. The goods yard, including the goods shed, was purchased by Mactaggart, Scott for use as a storage area, and fenced off. Instead of demolishing the shed, it was maintained by the company, for covered storage. The coal siding had served as the connection to the company's private sidings, and was was left *in situ*. While the signal box was demolished, the relay room, added as part of the 1961 signalling alterations, remained. The station building was taken over for use as a bothy for the track maintenance squad.

After these alterations the branch once again enjoyed a period of stability, apart from the loss of the scrap metal traffic from Gilmerton in 1978. However, in 1984 the very existence of the branch was put in jeopardy, with the strike by the National Union of Mineworkers, which started in February 1984 and lasted for 12 months. During this period the line lay dormant, apart from the annual visit from the weedkilling train in June 1984.

A major threat to the integrity of the trackbed materialised in the shape of the Edinburgh City Bypass, which had been planned since the 1930s. Fortunately, when the plans were prepared for the section between Burdiehouse and Sherrifhall, the branch was still in use and, therefore, the new road was carried over the line, thus avoiding the fate of the Waverley Route, further east, which has been completely severed. Ironically, the new bridge was brought into use in the latter part of 1988, when the branch had less than seven months of use left. Built immediately north of the site of Straiton Sidings, it has ensured that full use can be made of the trackbed in any future transport plans.

The decline of the deep mining industry in Britain, which had been under pressure from alternative energy sources for some time, continued after the settlement of the strike, and the announcement was made by British Coal (the successor to the NCB) that Bilston Glen would close in the summer of 1989.

While production had ceased, there were large reserves stockpiled on site, which had to be removed over the following two years. During this time the colliery was razed to the ground, and a new industrial park created on the part of the site nearest to the main road, while the remainder of the area remained derelict.

Chapter Nine

The Route Described

Although the branch extended to over eight miles in length, the geography of the area is such that almost every type of civil engineering construction was required to reach the terminus. With a ruling gradient of 1 in 55, it was no easy job for train crews, in either direction.

There had been a station at Millerhill since 1849, when the final section of the NBR Hawick branch opened. The alterations required to accommodate the branch traffic consisted of adding an additional bay on the west side of the existing down platform, with a run-round loop. The down side waiting room was converted to serve both platform faces, with a double canopy. A facing crossover on the main line was also put in, and a new signal box sited in the vee of the junction.

The branch leaves the main line in a cutting and swings west, passing under the road to Millerhill village (A6106). The overbridge carrying an old road, known as the Kaim, follows almost immediately, then the line enters open country on an embankment. The climb at 1 in 55 starts at this point, just short of the first milepost, and continues until Gilmerton station is reached. The village of Danderhall lies a short distance to the north of the line as it passes over the Edinburgh-Dalkeith road on a plate girder bridge. The line, which is now heading in a south-westerly direction, continues climbing on embankment through fields, past the site where a small platform would have been situated for the use of the Drum estate, the idea came to nothing. Soon the line, still at 1 in 55, passes under the first of the few entirely stone-built overbridges carrying the Edinburgh-Galashiels road and, still in cutting, approaches Gilmerton station, sited on a short stretch of 1 in 200. The colliery was on the down side only until 1928, when a new shaft was sunk on the opposite side, and a new set of sidings provided to deal with the increase in traffic. A steel overbridge, carrying narrow guage tracks, connected the original workings with the new. The single platform was on the down side, as was the small goods yard. The design of the station building followed that of the other stations on the branch, with the exception of Roslin. It consisted of two square brick-built 'wings' either side of the waiting room, which was constructed of timber. The brick portions could be increased in size if the location warranted, as at Loanhead. A grounded coach body was sited on the platform, next to the building, although its exact purpose is not clear. The yard consisted of two sidings, one serving the loading bank, on which was sited the 3 ton crane. Before the colliery was extended, it was served by a connection from the goods yard, involving a reversal, which must have hampered shunting operations. The siding ran behind the station building, and intending passengers had to cross it on the level to reach the booking office. After 1928 the original pit shaft was connected by the bridge already mentioned, and the connection from the goods yard removed. A small lamp room and a platelayers' hut completed the facilities, as traffic levels never warranted the provision of a goods shed.

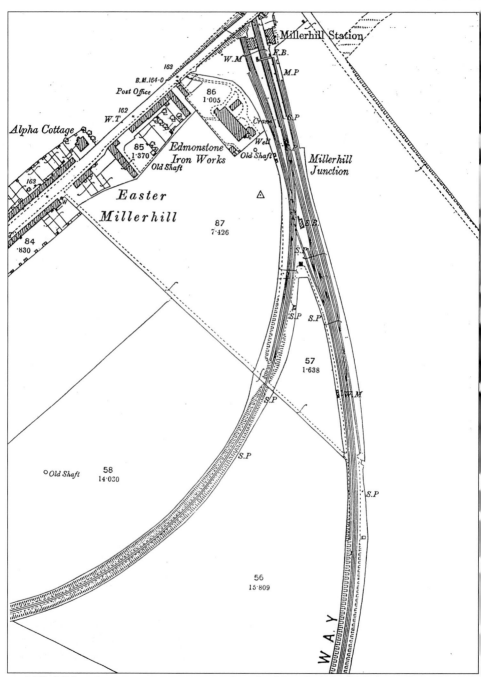

Millerhill Junction.   *Reproduced from the 25", 1896 Ordnance Survey Map*

A quiet moment at Millerhill Junction, looking north, on 17th April, 1955. Despite not having been used for over 20 years, the canopy is still in place in the branch bay platform.

C.J.B. Sanderson

Gilmerton in 1955, looking towards the junction, showing the final track layout and the freshly painted lamp hut on the left.   *C.J.B. Sanderson*

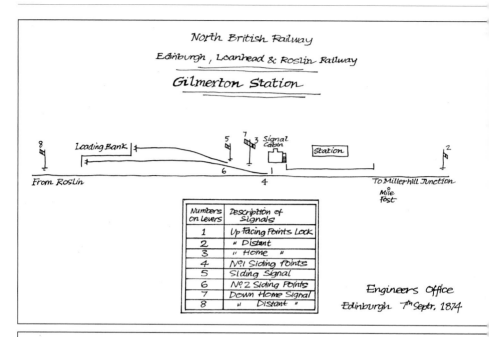

North British Railway

Edinburgh, Loanhead & Roslin Railway

Gilmerton Station

Numbers on Levers	Description of Signals
1	Up Facing Points Lock
2	" Distant "
3	" Home "
4	No.1 Siding Points
5	Siding Signal
6	No.2 Siding Points
7	Down Home Signal
8	" Distant "

Engineers Office
Edinburgh 7th Septr. 1874

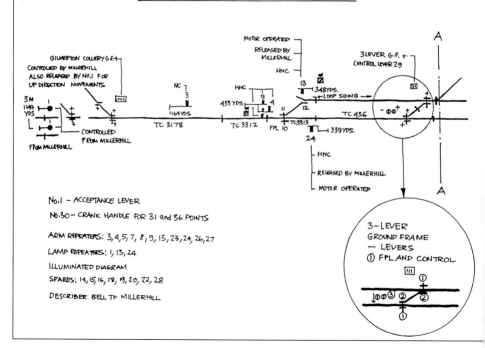

BRANCH SIGNALLING DIAGRAM 1961–1971·

No.1 – ACCEPTANCE LEVER

No.30 – CRANK HANDLE FOR 31 and 36 POINTS

ARM REPEATERS: 3,4,5,7, 8,9,13,23,24, 26,27

LAMP REPEATERS: 1, 13, 24

ILLUMINATED DIAGRAM

SPARES: 14,15,16, 18, 19, 20, 22, 28

DESCRIBER BELL TO MILLERHILL

3–LEVER
GROUND FRAME
– LEVERS
① FPL AND CONTROL

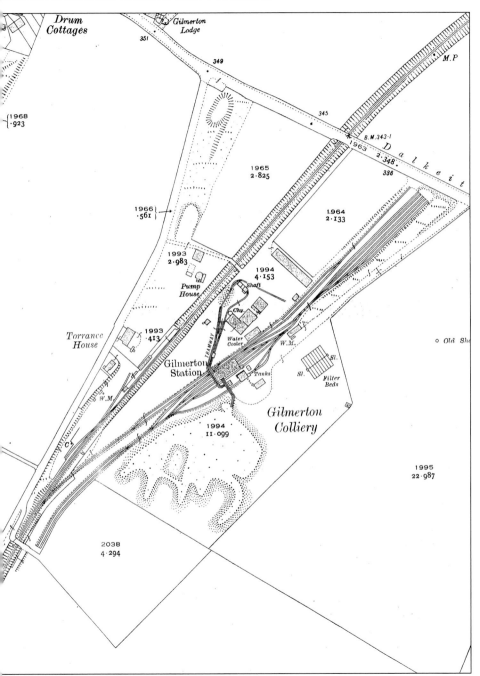

Gilmerton station. *Reproduced from the 25", 1932 Ordnance Survey Map*

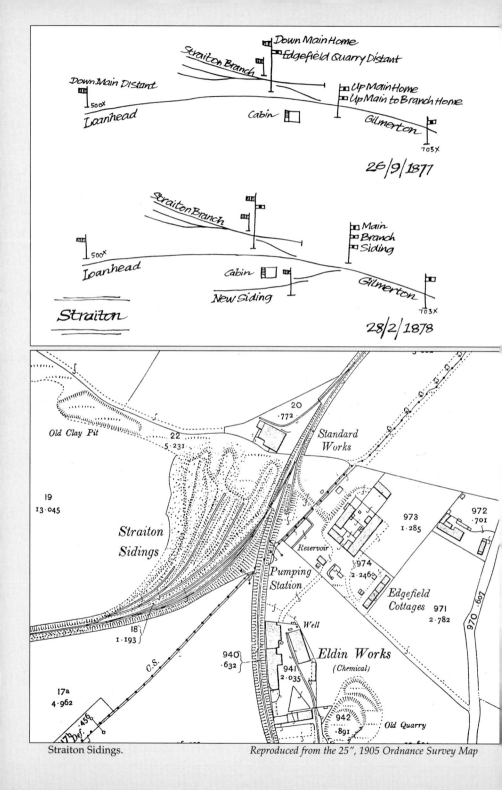

Straiton Sidings.

Reproduced from the 25", 1905 Ordnance Survey Map

The entry to the extensive sidings provided for the 1928 extension to the colliery on the up side of the line was controlled by a 4-lever ground frame, which also controlled a set of trap points sited opposite the passenger platform, to guard against runaways.

The 1 in 55 gradient starts again as the station is left behind, with trees on each side obscuring the view ahead. The Lasswade road is crossed by another plate girder bridge, the 13 ft 3 in. headroom necessitating the use of single deck buses on the Edinburgh-Polton route. Several vehicles have struck this bridge over the years, but have always come off worst. With West Edge farm up on the hill to the right, and the disused Melville Quarry over to the left, the line enters more open country, while the gradient eases to 1 in 100 before reaching the site of Straiton Sidings.

The mineral branch to Straiton curved away on the down side, on a rising gradient, and several loops were provided to cater for transfer traffic.

The line now curves to the left, and approaches the outskirts of Loanhead, passing the Eldin works on the up side, served by a single siding. Another standard cast-iron overbridge with stone abutments carries the line under Edgefield road, the farm of the same name coming into view on the left as the curve straightens out. Originally at this point, on the down side, there stood a signal box named Edgefield Weighs, controlling the north connection to Ramsey Colliery sidings. Occasionally the 'pug' could be seen using this part of the colliery track, if a long rake of wagons had to be drawn out. It was usually found further on, positioning wagons in the sidings at the south end, which were on a rising gradient, to enable them to be run by gravity through the 'winder'. This raised whichever end of the wagon was opposite the end door, tipping the contents into an underground bunker, from where the coal was raised up to the washer. The now empty wagon then ran on to be marshalled for refilling at the pithead, to continue the process.

The line, curving once again to the right, skirts the pit bing on an embankment and enters Loanhead station, passing the engineering works of Mactaggart, Scott, which had been established in 1898, below the line on the left. The company specialises in designing and manufacturing marine hydraulic machinery, principally for the navies of the world, and is still very much in business today. The goods yard was further on, on the same side of the line, with a connection from the loop. In common with many other NBR branch line stations, the single platform was situated on the main line, beyond the loop. In contrast to Gilmerton, the station was within easy reach of the centre of the town, with ready access via Station Road. The station building was of similar design to that at Gilmerton, but with increased accommodation. The station master's house adjoined, at right angles. The yard contained a standard NBR goods shed and a 5-ton crane, with a weighbridge just inside the entrance from Station Road.

The line enters a cutting immediately after leaving the platform end, on a short stretch of 1 in 60 and, opposite the southern connection to the Ramsey loop, stood the locomotive water tank. This consisted of a rectangular rivetted tank on two concrete beams supported by two brick piers at the trackside, and by the side of the cutting at the opposite end. The line then runs under the

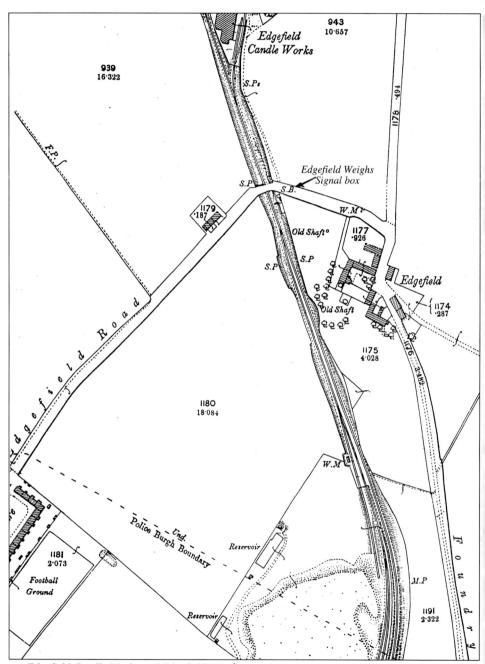

Edgefield Candle Works and Edgefield Weighs signal box.

Reproduced from the 25", 1907 Ordnance Survey Map

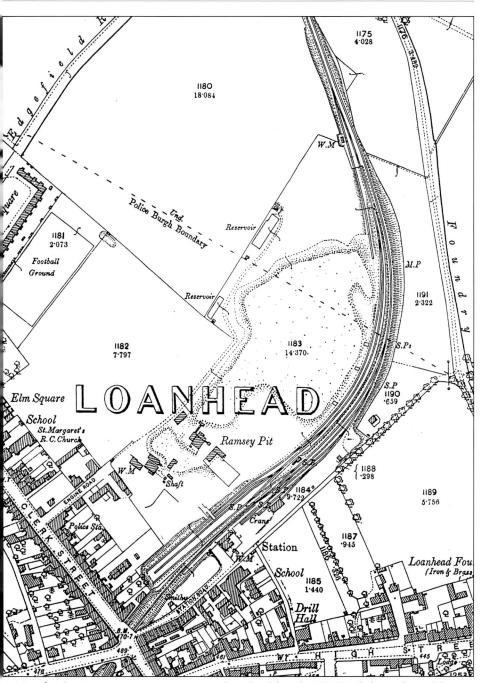

Loanhead station.   *Reproduced from the 25", 1896 Ordnance Survey Map*

Loanhead Signal box

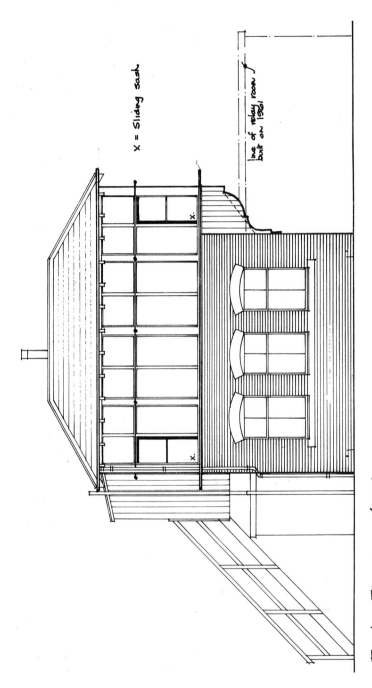

X = Sliding sash

line of relay room ↗
built on 1961

Front Elevation (S.E.)

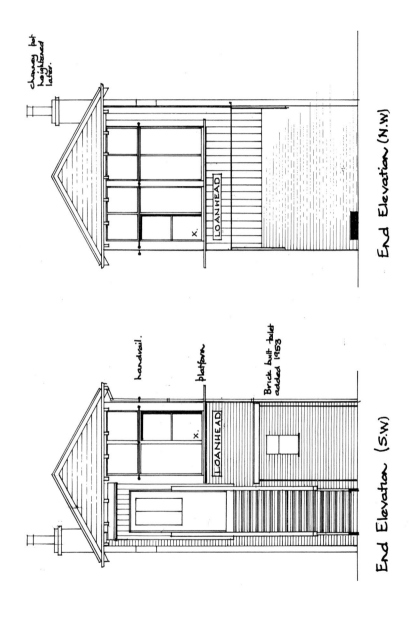

chimney pot
heightened
later.

LOANHEAD

x.

End Elevation (N.W)

handrail.

platform

Brick built toilet
added 1953

LOANHEAD

x.

End Elevation (S.W)

Loanhead Goods Shed

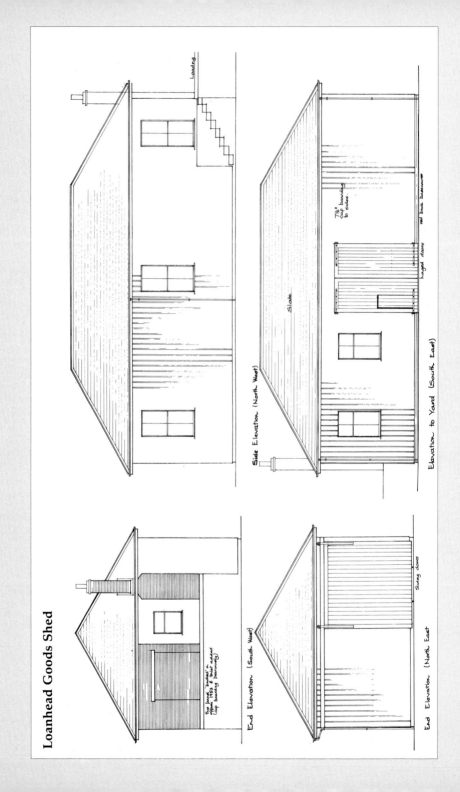

End Elevation (South West)

Side Elevation (North West)

Slate

End Elevation (North East)

Elevation to Yard (South East)

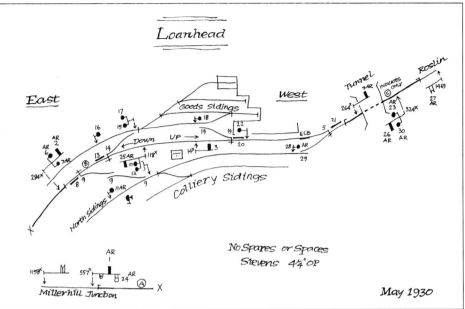

Loanhead

May 1930

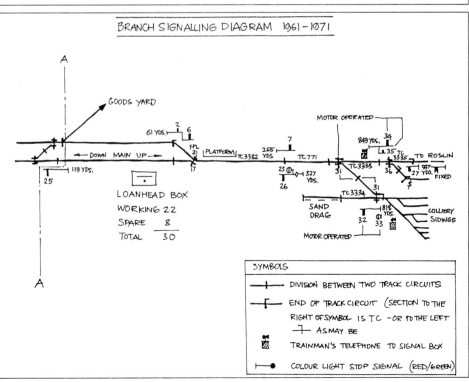

BRANCH SIGNALLING DIAGRAM   1961 - 1071

LOANHEAD BOX
WORKING 22
SPARE   8
TOTAL   30

SYMBOLS

DIVISION BETWEEN TWO TRACK CIRCUITS

END OF TRACK CIRCUIT (SECTION TO THE RIGHT OF SYMBOL IS TC - OR TO THE LEFT AS MAY BE

TRAINMAN'S TELEPHONE TO SIGNAL BOX

COLOUR LIGHT STOP SIGNAL (RED/GREEN)

Loanhead Station

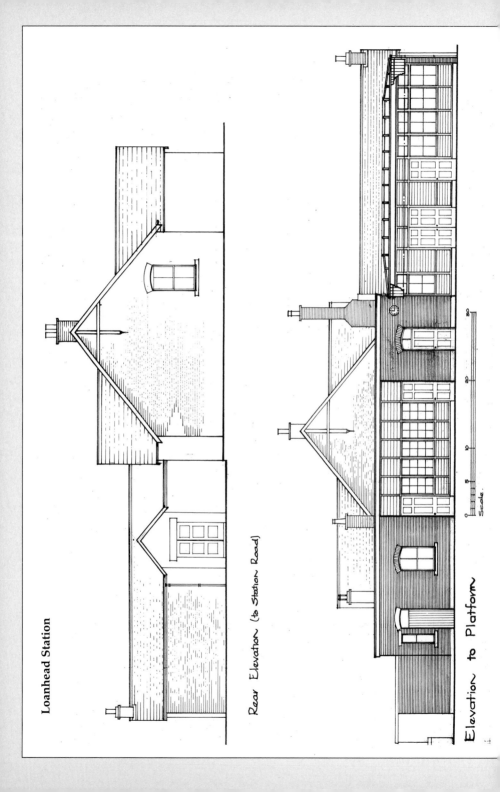

Rear Elevation (to Station Road)

Elevation to Platform

Scale.

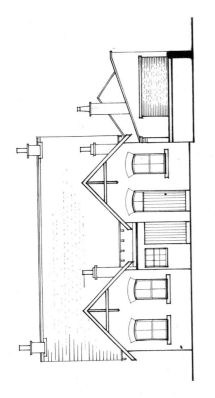

End Elevation (North West)

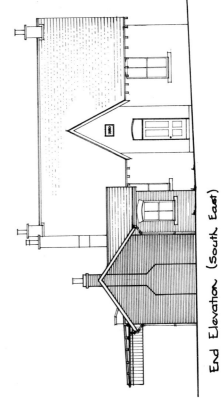

End Elevation (South East)

Loanhead Station

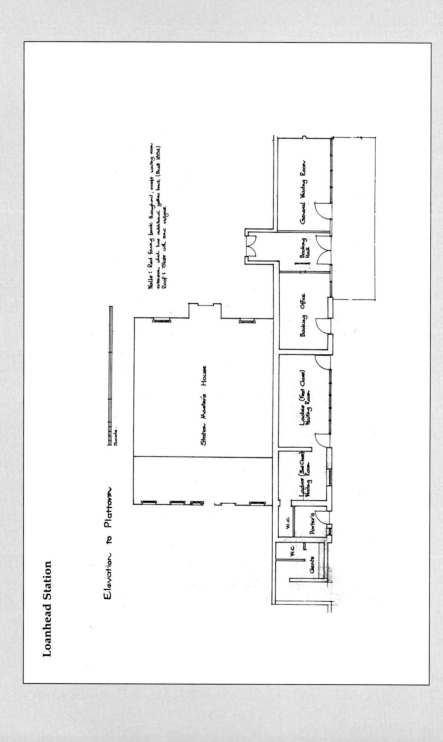

Elevation to Platform

Scale:

Station Master's House

Walls: Red facing brick throughout, except wating room extension which has additional yellow brick (Built 1824)
Roof: Slate with zinc ridges.

General Waiting Room

Booking Hall

Booking Office

Ladies (First Class) Waiting Room

Ladies (2nd Class) Waiting Room

W.C.

Porter's

W.C.

Gents

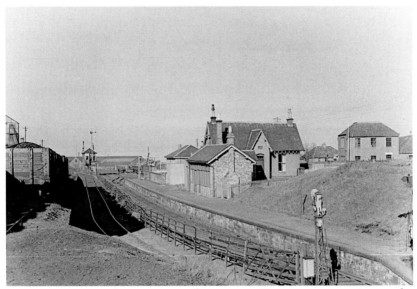

A general view of Loanhead, taken from the Ramsey Colliery sidings, in April, 1955. The
loaded wagons will be run by gravity to the washer, just visible above the last wagon.
C.J.B. Sanderson

junction of Clerk Street and The Loan by means of the first of the two 'tunnels'
on the branch. At 47 yards long, it is technically a bridge, as the official
definition of a tunnel is any structure over the railway longer than 54 yards, but
it appears as such in the LNER 'Statement of Tunnels'.

Emerging from the tunnel, the gradient levels out and the line is in a narrow
cutting, with stone retaining walls on each side, almost immediately passing
under Burghlee Terrace, known locally as the 'Back Loan', by another stone and
cast-iron bridge, this time built on a skew. The line continues in cutting, with
the local cemetery on the left, before the connection to Bilston Glen Colliery
swings away to the right. The original connection to Burghlee Colliery at this
point was completely obliterated by the new sidings and headshunt provided
for the opening in 1961 of Bilston Glen Colliery.

Continuing south, the line is taken across the valley of Bilston Burn by the
impressive single-span bridge, 150 feet above the stream at its highest point.
Having gained the other side of the glen, the character of the countryside
changes, leaving industry behind, and the line passes at 1 in 110 through the
dense woodland of the Dryden estate. Emerging into more open country, the
line follows a minor road in the direction of Roslin, first passing over, and then
under twice, in a series of gentle reverse curves, before reaching Roslin station.

As befitted the original terminus of the line, Roslin differed from Gilmerton
and Loanhead by having the single platform on the loop, and a much more
substantially-built station building with a slate roof. Roslin station building
barely survived its final closure, being burnt as the result of vandalism, later in

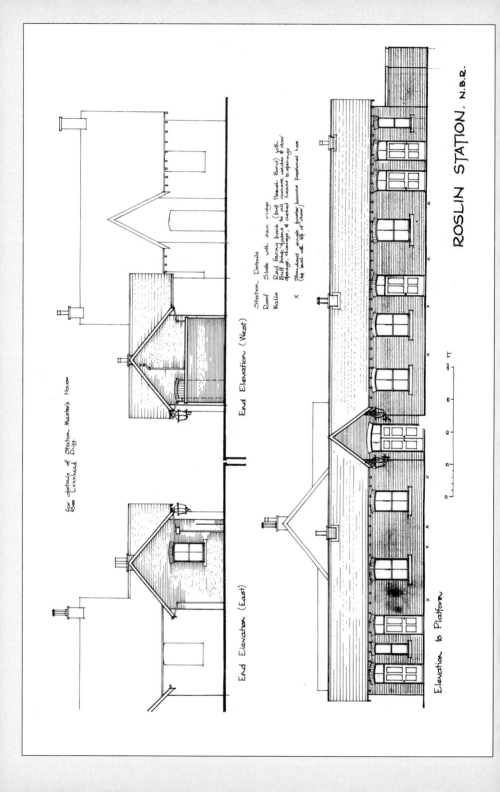

ROSLIN STATION. N.B.R.

For details of Station Master's House
See Loanhead Dwg.

End Elevation (West)

End Elevation (East)

Station Details

Roof   Slate with zinc ridge
Walls   Red facing brick (built Flemish Bond) with
            buff brick pilasters to all corners, window & door
            openings changes of arched heads to openings
      X   Stringed single pantry boarded fenced here
            (up seat sill top of door)

Elevation to Platform

0   5   10   15   20 FT

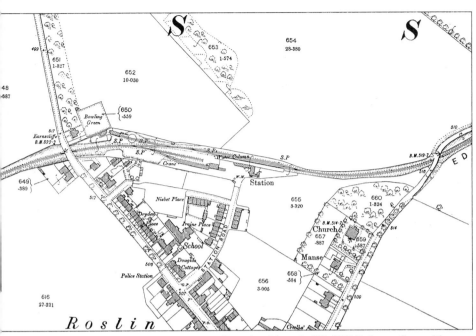

Roslin station.

Reproduced from the 25″, 1896 Ordnance Survey Map

Roslin Colliery branch.

Reproduced from the 25″, 1907 Ordnance Survey Map

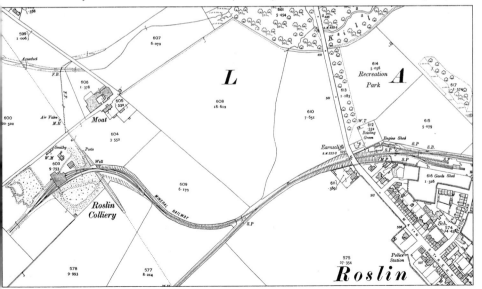

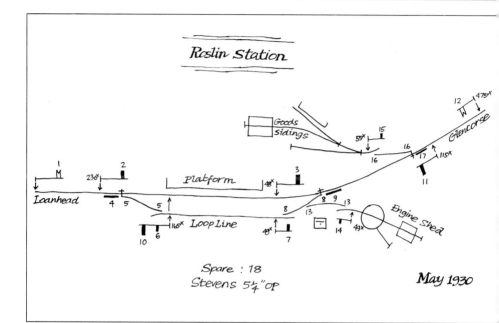

Roslin Station

Goods Sidings

Platform

Loanhead

Loop Line

Spare : 18
Stevens 5¼"op

May 1930

Roslin appears devoid of any form of traffic in this 1955 view, indicating that the days of the goods service were numbered.   *C.J.B. Sanderson*

Glencorse viaduct is lit by the late afternoon sun in July 1959. *Ray Montgomery*

Glencorse in 1955, showing the familiar layout of station building with the house at right angles. By this time the wooden section of the building had been removed. *C.J.B. Sanderson*

Glencorse station.

Reproduced from the 25", 1894 Ordnance Survey Map

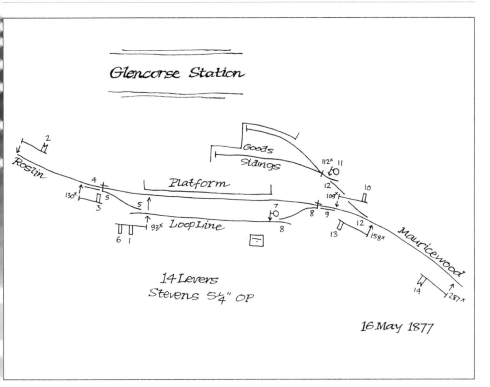

Glencorse Station

14 Levers
Stevens 5¼" OP

16 May 1877

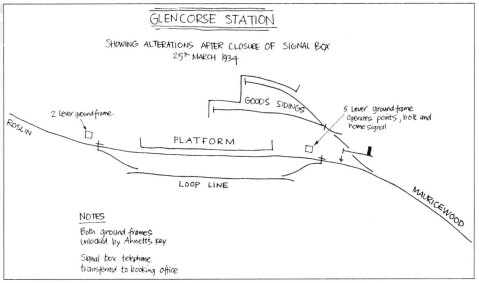

GLENCORSE STATION

SHOWING ALTERATIONS AFTER CLOSURE OF SIGNAL BOX
25ᵗʰ MARCH 1934

NOTES

Both ground frames
unlocked by Ahnett's key

Signal box telephone
transferred to booking office

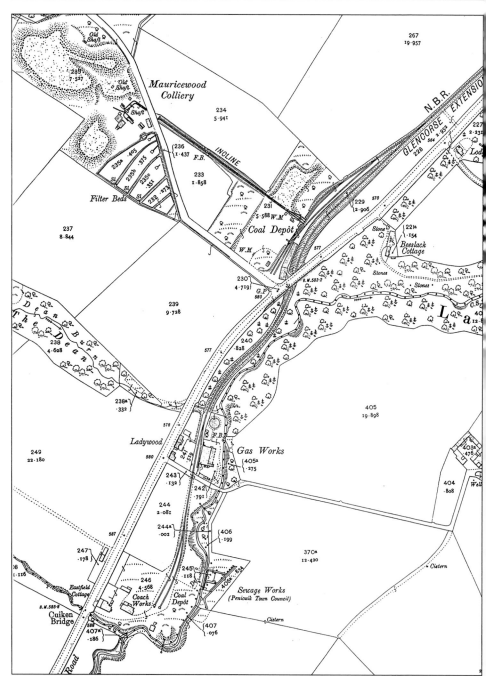

The end of the branch.

Reproduced from the 25", 1896 Ordnance Survey Map

1959, and subsequently demolished. As at Loanhead, a station master's house was provided, at right angles to the platform. The small goods yard had only three sidings, one serving the goods shed. The branch passenger locomotive was kept here, in a small shed accessed from the turntable road, together with a short siding for locomotive coal and ash wagons. All of these facilities appear to have been removed by 1935. An adjacent water tank on a brick base originally fed two columns, one at the shed itself and the other at the south end of the platform.

The Glencorse Extension, to use its official title, continued southward, under the Bilston-Roslin road and passed Roslin Colliery, served by a short branch on the down side. Known locally as the Moat Pit, after a local farm, it was set incongrously in a rural area, with no other heavy industry visible for several miles around. After passing under the south road to Roslin and over a minor road, the line turned to the south-west, following the valley of the river South Esk, passed under the Auchendinny road and entered the golf course. The golf club was not established until 1890, the land being part of Milton Mill farm before this date. A public right-of-way crossed the line of the railway here by means of an iron footbridge on brick piers. Entering a wood, the line suddenly burst out into the small valley of the Glencorse Burn, crossed by the 15-arch viaduct, constructed in local brick from Whitehill, near Rosewell. The gradient steepened to 1 in 70 once again on leaving the viaduct, through the 44 yards-long 'tunnel' under the Edinburgh-Penicuik road to reach the passenger terminus at Glencorse.

Situated directly opposite the barracks, the single platform contained the now familiar brick and timber building with the station house at right-angles. The 17-lever signal box was situated opposite the south end of the platform, on the other side of the loop. Only two goods sidings were provided, one serving a loading bank, the other the 3-ton crane.

The mineral branch continued on towards Penicuik, the siding serving Mauricewood Colliery branching off to the right, while the main line continued on down a 1 in 100 gradient and over reverse curves to pass under the main road again, then up a short stretch of 1 in 70 to the gasworks siding. The single siding was on the up side, and relied on a scotch block rather than catch points to protect the main line. A small wagon weighbridge was also provided.

The line continued on, crossing the road to Eastfield farm on the level, to reach Eastfield. The crossing gates were operated by the train crew, and were normally kept closed over the railway. After the attempts to open the colliery were abandoned, a coal depot was established, operated by the SIC. The loop was removed and two sidings provided, wagons being propelled from Glencorse.

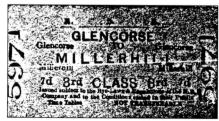

NBR third class ticket.   *Courtesy Douglas Blades*

In a scene reminiscent of branch line photographs of the 1950s, with rusty rails stretching into the distance, Loanhead station is pictured on a sunny day in August 1995.   *Author*

Thanks to regular maintenance by the present owners, Loanhead goods shed carries its 125 years well, as can be seen in this August 1997 view.   *Author*

Chapter Ten

The Present Day

With the removal of the Bilston Glen traffic, it was assumed generally that the trackbed of the line would soon join the ranks of the many abandoned branches throughout the country, but this proved not to be the case. It had been intended to remove the track for re-use on a project in Ayrshire, but this came to nothing, and with privatisation imminent, the cost of removal was not justifiable without a definite use for the materials.

The line slumbered on, gradually disappearing under the relentless covering of weeds and the inevitable domestic rubbish and old car doors. Its value as a walkway, which had always been seen by some of the local population, became more widespread, although the really useful section over the viaduct had to be securely blocked off, due to the dangerous condition of the decking. It had usually been possible to force a way around the barriers at either end of the viaduct, but a permanent solution had to be found to protect the public.

All this time the line was offically 'open' as far as British Rail was concerned. In 1985 the Lothian Region had published its Structure Plan, outlining the Local Authority's strategy for the future. Included in the Transport section was the pleasing news that the remaining part of the line had been safeguarded for use as an addition to the existing network of abandoned railways which have been turned into cycleways, and also for inclusion in possible public transport schemes sometime in the future. This policy was re-affirmed in 1994, and the announcement was made in October 1998 that Midlothian Council had instigated a £15,000 Feasibility Study into the reopening of the line to Loanhead for passenger traffic.

A sleeper has been secured across the track at the Kaim overbridge, to mark the limit of Railtrack ownership. At Privatisation, the remainder of the line up to the exchange siding at Bilston Glen, including the track itself, passed to Rail Property Services (RPS), formerly the British Rail Property Board. In 1998, ownership changed hands once more to Sustrans, who are responsible for many of the cycleways in the area.

Starting at the junction, we shall now cover the route of the branch, describing the situation in 1999.

The closure of the foundry adjacent to the site of Millerhill station enabled the neighbouring builder's merchants to purchase the site for expansion, removing all traces of the foundry in the process. A new road was constructed to provide an independent access to the former BR loco depot, currently operated by Transrail (West). This crosses the spur, which served Monktonhall Colliery, on the level, with trains being handsignalled over the crossing. The branch was used by locomotives working the colliery up to its closure in 1997, as far as the home signal (No. M27), in order to clear the track circuit. The track is severed 100 metres south of this point by a pipeline trench which was dug across the line shortly after the running of the last train. Instead of adopting the more usual method of tunnelling through the embankment, two rail lengths were removed

Bridge No. 3 carries the branch over the Edinburgh-Dalkeith (A7) road. The masonry replaced after the 1977 accident, described in the text, can be seen clearly in this view, taken on 31st August, 1997.   *Author*

Bridge No. 2 shows little sign of being 125 years old when photographed in August 1997. Built on a slight skew, it owes its longevity to the lack of traffic on the farm road it carries over the line.   *Author*

and the embankment dug out to accommodate the pipe. The embankment was not restored, leaving a 48 metre gap in the track. From here, the line is clear (albeit overgrown in certain places) to Bilston viaduct. Some chairs have been removed by vandals near the site of Gilmerton station and the Bypass bridge. The bridge over the Lasswade road was struck once again by a road vehicle during the summer of 1998, and subsequently raised some 18 inches by the insertion of steel beams under the span. This has enabled Lothian Regional Transport to use double-deck buses on their No. 80 service for the first time.

Loanhead station has survived best of all, with many buildings and features still visible. The goods shed is externally complete, having been maintained by Mactaggart, Scott, as explained in Chapter Eight. Apart from some minor alterations in the area of the office, the only items missing from the interior are the wooden crane (which may have been removed sometime before sale) and a length of track. The coal merchant's siding still exists, including the buffer stop, and is used for storage of heavy items of equipment. The station house had been in the possession of a model railway enthusiast for some years and, when the remaining part of the station building was put up for sale by the British Railways Property Board, he took the opportunity to purchase, to ensure that the building would be preserved in its present form. Some original internal features survive, such as the ticket window and barrier, although much of the interior suffered during its period as the platelayers' bothy, as some of the wooden interior panelling has disappeared. The platform, which was not included in the sale, is in good order, considering the amount of undergrowth in evidence. The next features encountered comprise the south connection to the Ramsey Colliery and the pillars which supported the water tank, again much overgrown. The two bridges in the centre of Loanhead are standing up well to levels of traffic never envisaged in the last century, while the retaining walls of the cutting which connects the two are also in good condition. Reaching the former junction of the Burghlee/Bilston Glen sidings, apart from a crossover and two signal posts on Sustrans property, there is very little evidence of the large number of lines which once served both collieries. Of Bilston Glen Colliery itself, no trace remains, and a newly-built business park is gradually occupying the site. A little further on, Bilston viaduct can be seen stretching out over the glen, as impressive as ever.

Midlothian District Council commissioned a report in January 1994 on the category 'A' listed viaduct, with a view to reopening it for pedestrians and cycle traffic, following the success of the refurbishment of Glenesk Bridge near Dalkeith. Carried out by Blyth & Blyth of Edinburgh, it disclosed that the structure was in good condition considering the period of disuse, and that the main problem lay in the deck, which would require replacing with one strong enough to take maintenance vehicles. The present parapets are too low, and would have to be replaced with a more suitable design to protect pedestrians. The total cost of all improvements was originally estimated at £515,000, with the option of demolition at £280,000. As always, finding the necessary funds was a problem, but the announcement in March 1997 that the project would to go ahead was well received both locally and nationally. Ownership passed to the Edinburgh Green Belt Trust, who were awarded a £212,000 Heritage Lottery Fund Grant, to assist in the project. Accommodating recent changes in Health and Safety Regulations resulted in escalation of the total cost of the project to 1.3 million pounds. A viewing platform will be provided at the north-east corner of the site, and an access will be created from Station Road, Loanhead, which will provide a quiet walk through the centre of the busy town.

To the south of Bilston viaduct, as is to be expected due to the longer period of disuse, some areas have changed out of all recognition, but a large proportion of the trackbed remains and can be traced, with some searching.

The first section has been in regular use as a footpath and is passable until just before bridge No. 15 is reached. The metal span has been removed, either to reduce maintenance costs or to remove the height restriction to farm traffic. The path bypasses the bridge by the nearby single track road. From here almost to the site of Roslin station, while intact, the *solum* of the line has become overgrown with bushes and mature trees. Overbridges 16 and 17 still stand, the cast iron beams and parapets well preserved, as is the stonework, considering their age.

Some 200 metres to the south, the line has been breached by a small housing development which now occupies the station site. From the former station entrance a footpath skirts the houses on the left, and passes under the Bilston road overbridge by means of a corrugated tube, the remaining space being filled with concrete, for road traffic strengthening purposes. The path follows the curve of the line, skirting a large private housing estate built right up to the lineside fence in 1971, and bears off to the right, following the line of the Roslin Colliery connection. All traces of the colliery were removed by a land reclamation scheme in the early 1980s. From the point where the path diverges, until the B7003 is reached, the trackbed is almost impassable due to trees and undergrowth. Bridge No. 19 has been completely removed and the road re-aligned. A row of trees marks the course of the line on the south side of the road for about ¼ mile, from where the entire area has been obliterated by a huge sand quarry, owned by Tarmac Ltd. This work extends to just short of the site of bridge No. 20, which has also completely disappeared. The next section had been restored to farmland after the track was lifted and remained so until 1995, when a golf range was constructed over the route. When road improvements to the adjacent A701 were undertaken in 1970, the overbridge carrying the B7026 was removed at the same time, to ease the road gradient up from Auchendinny village.

The only indication of the line of route through the golf course can be gauged from the seventh hole, called 'The Railway', although there is very little evidence now to show that trains once posed an extra hazard to players. The public right-of-way from Auchendinny to Milton Bridge has been restored to its original route, before the building of the railway, with the removal of the footbridge (suggested by the Board of Trade), which lasted until 1971. The northern approach to Glencorse viaduct runs through a thick wood, and can just be traced with difficulty, as a thick wood covers the area. When it was announced in 1986 that the viaduct, a Grade A listed structure, had been declared unsafe and that Glencorse Golf Club could not meet the cost of restoration, estimated at that time to cost £250,000, a great deal of debate ensued.

The viaduct and the portion of the trackbed through the golf course had remained the property of British Rail until the late 1970s, when it was offered for sale. As the club was anxious to own the entire area, and there was a possibility that the BR land could have been used as a landfill site for refuse, the decision was made to purchase all of the property on offer, including the viaduct.

All went well until 1986 when bricks, dislodged by water and frost damage, were found below one of the arches. As golfers passed under the structure at least twice while playing the course, an immediate survey was carried out and netting was rigged up to protect the players. To effect immediate repairs would cost £250,000, with no guarantee against further deterioration. The club, which was very keen to retain the viaduct, as it had been in existence longer that the golf course itself and formed the centre piece of the club badge, did not have funds to meet the cost of repairs, nor could any way be found to raise the money in time. Accordingly, at an Extraordinary General Meeting held in January 1987, the membership reluctantly voted to seek permission to have the viaduct demolished. This was granted by Midlothian District Council Planning Committee, and tenders were sought, after the Army declined to carry out the job as an exercise. The contract was awarded to Messrs McDonald of Selkirk, who bored nine holes packed with 13 lb. of gelignite into each pier. The date for the demolition was set for 1st May, 1987 and a large crowd of onlookers that had gathered had to be kept at a safe distance.

The contractors had carried out their job well, and the structure fell exactly where intended, with a minimum of damage to the golf course. The rubble was bulldozed into areas prepared beforehand and covered with topsoil and, with the passage of time, it is hard to spot any trace today, apart from a few sections of brickwork uncovered by erosion from the Glencorse Burn. The whin bushes which have been planted over each side of the exposed ends of the embankments give the only clue to where the viaduct stood for over 110 years.

On 26th August, 1995, the rails are completely obscured by undergrowth, and the 'tunnel' under the centre of Loanhead is only just visible beyond the supports of the water tank.
Author

The detail of the infill to bridge No. 17 at Roslin, carried out on the conversion to a walkway.
Author

A single sleeper marks the limit of Railtrack property, at bridge No. 2. The photograph was taken on 31st August, 1997.
Author

The short section of trackbed from the south end of the viaduct and bridge No. 24 under the Penicuik road are in good order, apart from the inevitable saplings, as this section is in the ownership of the golf club. The 'tunnel' is in excellent condition, with very little signs of graffitti or rubbish dumping, probably due to its situation, some distance from the nearest houses and close to Glencorse Infantry Depot. The presence of the Army is also a factor in relation to the lack of development of Glencorse station site. After closure the area lay derelict for some years, until bought by the Ministry of Defence, who converted the northern half into a vehicle park, leaving the platform edge and the adjcent trackbed intact. The remaining part, comprising the rest of the goods yard and the trackbed up to the road to Greenlaw Mains farm, has been landscaped by the local council and planted with shrubs and bushes. A tarmacadam footpath forms a pleasant alternative to the normal pavement, while the pivot post of the goods yard crane remains, albeit painted a peculiar shade of pink. The path rejoins the pavement at the Greenlaw Mains farm road, where the southern abutment is all that survives of the low overbridge.

Apart from a short section immediately south of the bridge abutment, the rest of the branch has disappeared, due to land redevelopment and road improvements. Mauricewood Primary School occupies the area up to the site of the underbridge, all traces of which have been removed and the road re-aligned. Thereafter a small industrial estate has replaced the gasworks, with the access road joining the public road at the former level crossing. No trace of the coal depot remains, as various changes in the use of the area have taken place over the years, the latest being a large supermarket.

With the restoration of Bilston viaduct and the possibility of the Millerhill-Loanhead section once again playing a part in Midlothian's public transport network, the future appears bright for the branch.

The substantial bridge which carries the A720 Edinburgh City bypass over the branch has safeguarded the trackbed for the future; 14th February, 1999.   *Author*

To illustrate the NBR class 'R' 0-6-0 tanks first used on the branch, this view of No. 1335 is offered, in place of No. 241.   *Author's Collection*

No photographs of 'R' class 4-4-0T No. 104 have come to light, but this view of No. 10458 at St Margaret's Shed in LNER days shows the distinctive lines of this diminutive class.
G.N. Heathcote

Chapter Eleven

Trains and Traffic

With the survival of a considerable portion of the branch into the late 1980s, the full spectrum of motive power has been used, from the steam locomotives of the 1870s to 1,750 hp class '37' diesels. If the latter day use of the stub of the branch at Millerhill is considered, 2,400 hp class '56' locomotives can also be included.

All locomotives and rolling stock were provided by the NBR under the working agreement, with St Margaret's Shed supplying the locomotives. These arrangements continued through the LNER era into British Railways days, except that Seafield Shed (a sub-shed of St Margaret's) tended to provide the motive power for the mineral turns, followed by Haymarket and Millerhill depots after dieselisation.

Passenger Services

It was common for the same locomotive to be the 'branch engine' for a considerable number of years, except for periodic maintenance, such as boiler washing out and major overhaul. Photographs of the early branch locomotives have proved impossible to find, and those which do exist are mainly of 'foreign' examples. This may be due to the novelty of spotting an unusual locomotive on the service.

Details of the locomotives and passenger rolling stock used at the time of the opening have defied exhaustive research, as the usual accounts of the opening day celebrations are absent. It may have been that, considering the delays to the opening date, both the ELR and the NBR were anxious to get on with running the railway. In any event, the usual festivities appear to have been dispensed with. Whatever stock was used, it would have consisted of the usual spartan four-wheeled vehicles favoured by the NBR at that time.

The introduction of NBR class 'R' (LNER 'J82') 0-6-0Ts in 1875-6, to augment the Wheatley 0-6-0 saddle tanks (NBR class 'E') on many local branches, provide the first clue, as their designer, Dugald Drummond, followed the practice of his former employer (the London, Brighton and South Coast Railway) in naming each member of the class after places served by the NBR. Thus No. 241 carried the name *Roslin* painted on the side tanks.

The next type of locomotive used on the branch also carried the name for a short time after its introduction in 1881. This was No. 104, NBR class 'R' (LNER 'D51'), one of Drummond's neat 4-4-0Ts. Drummond having moved to the Caledonian Railway in 1882, his successor, Matthew Holmes, quickly set about removing the names, on the grounds that intending passengers mistook them for destination boards, with occasional embarrassing results for all concerned. As the line was extended to Glencorse some five years earlier it might have appeared logical to have altered the locomotive name to suit.

A typical branch train of the period immediately before the Grouping, in charge of class 'P' 0-4-4T
No. 1327, passes Portobello.   *G.N. Heathcote*

Class 'G7' 0-4-4T No. 90 pauses for the photographer in the loop at Glencorse terminus, in NBR
days.   *Rae Montgomery*

No. 104 was destined to be the branch passenger engine for over 30 years, being involved in the fatal accident of 2nd July, 1912. Although it was not badly damaged in the accident, it may be that the NBR decided that this class was not suitable for the line, as the engine was replaced shortly after this date.

No. 104's successor was the more powerful No. 1327, NBR class 'P' (LNER 'G8'), an 0-4-4T. One of a class of six engines built in 1877, they were originally 0-4-2Ts. They had been transferred from the Glasgow area, having themselves been replaced by W.P. Reid's 4-4-2 passenger tanks (LNER class 'C15'). As with Nos. 241 and 104, it had carried the names *Gareloch* and *Ladybank* before 1883. Not renumbered by the LNER, it was scrapped in May 1925, after 48 years' service.

The replacement was also a 0-4-4T, No. 354, NBR class 'M' (LNER 'G9'), which lasted until the withdrawal of passenger services. The class 'M' tanks were the last class of 0-4-4Ts built for the NBR, and were to be found on most of the Midlothian branches at this period. When photographed at Roslin in 1925, it still carried NBR livery, and was withdrawn in September 1936.

The passenger locomotives were allocated to St Margaret's, and sub-shedded at Roslin, to provide the early morning and late evening services to and from Edinburgh.

The 1875 timetable shows a service for 1st, 2nd and 4th class passengers of four trains each way, commencing with the 8.35 am from Roslin, and the last returning at 8.58 pm. This basic service remained in use right up until closure, with one additional return trip after the Glencorse extension opened, plus extra Saturdays-only services introduced prior to World War I. Up trains were allowed 38 minutes to reach Roslin from Edinburgh in 1875, and 45 minutes in the opposite direction.

After the line was extended to Glencorse, an extra five and three minutes respectively were allowed, and an operating change was made, whereby several services ran from Edinburgh combined with those to Polton or Penicuik. Despite the provision of a bay platform at Millerhill, none of the trains is shown as terminating there. Some complicated shunting must have been necessary at Millerhill to split and remarshal the coaches, not to mention the increased risk of passengers boarding the wrong part of the train.

The popularity of Roslin and its surroundings has already been explained, and to cope with the increase in passengers, extra vehicles were added to the regular services or complete sets of coaches allocated. Monday 16th April, 1900, for example, was a public holiday in Glasgow as well as Edinburgh and Leith (a separate town at that time). All trains were strengthened by additional coaches, and not combined at Millerhill. To cater for the evening rush, 14 vehicles from the Stirling and Perth service, due at Waverley at 4.15 pm were allocated to the 6.20 pm Glencorse train, returning at 7.30. The stock was then to run empty to Corstorphine.

Two views of a military train on 4th July, 1959, in the care of 'J37' class 0-6-0 No. 64577 and 'J38' 0-6-0 No. 65915. *Above:* No. 64577 has detached and run into the loop, allowing No. 65915 to draw the rear of the train clear of the north loop points. *Below:* The locomotives have just completed running round their train. The leading Gresley full brake was used to carry the band's instruments (*see page 74*).   *(Both) Rae Montgomery*

Special Passenger Workings

The branch was visited by at least four special trains run for railway enthusiasts, beginning with one of the earliest, on Saturday 28th April, 1951. Hauled by 'D34' class 4-4-0 *Glen Falloch*, it was organised by the Stephenson Locomotive Society and also visited South Queensferry. By coincidence, the next special, on 29th August, 1959, utilised another 'D34', the restored *Glen Douglas* (NBR No. 256, BR No. 62469). This was the last opportunity for enthusiasts to reach Glencorse, before the line was cut back to Roslin, as explained in Chapter Seven. Another restored 4-4-0 locomotive, ex-Great North of Scotland Railway *Gordon Highlander* (GNSR No. 49, BR No. 62277) was the chosen motive power for the last steam-hauled special, which reached Roslin on 16th October, 1965. By the autumn of 1967, when the penultimate special ran on 7th October, a class '101' dmu was provided. This train also visited Leith Citadel, Granton and Haddington, finishing with a trip over the Suburban Circle.

Military specials were common, continuing up to 1959, when on Saturday 4th July the Royal Scots Territorials were conveyed to their summer camp at Sennybridge in South Wales. The train was double-headed by 'J37' No. 64577 and 'J38' No. 65915, and consisted of at least 12 Gresley bogie coaches, a lengthy train, which resulted in some complicated shunting at the terminus.

Goods and Mineral Services

Introduction

Before describing the freight service on the branch, a description of how goods train working was carried out prior to the late 1960s will be useful to those unfamiliar with the process.

All trains today are 'continuously braked' that is, they move as one unit, and the braking effort is controlled by the driver and applied to all vehicles throughout the train. From the earliest days of railways, wagons were coupled together by a simple three link coupling dropped over a hook on the adjacent wagon, without any means of keeping the vehicles tight together. This meant that, on starting, each wagon moved independently as the couplings became taut, and, depending on the number of wagons on a train, the locomotive could be travelling at 5 to 10 miles an hour by the time the brake van started to move. The danger of breaking a coupling was very great, especially in the early days, as some of the materials used were of doubtful quality. An experienced train crew could minimise these problems by carefully taking up the slack on starting and allowing the wagons to come together gradually when braking. This was possible only by learning all the gradients on each particular stretch of line, and by the display of considerable skill and co-operation between the locomotive crew and the guard. Only the brakes on the engine and brake van were under the direct control of the crew; although each wagon was fitted with a brake operated by a handlever and secured by a pin (the process being known as 'pinning down brakes'), these could only be properly applied while stationary.

Before descending a gradient which was too steep for the locomotive and van brakes to control, the train had to come to a stand while the guard, using his experience, pinned down as many wagon brakes as was thought necessary to control the speed during the descent, leaving the locomotive and van brakes in reserve. Performing this operation on a dark night in a downpour was no easy task, as can be imagined. The engine crew did not have an easy time either, as often locomotives ran tender first on the return journey,with only a canvas storm sheet stretched between the rear of the cab and the tender top to protect the men from the elements.

On the Glencorse branch, trains would stop near Straiton Sidings to pin down the brakes, although locomotives could still have steam on crossing the Lasswade road bridge, before descending the 1 in 55 gradient. The train then had to be dragged down the initial part of the gradient, and the speed on the descent controlled with the brakes on the locomotive and brake van. If the guard applied too many brakes, the train might be brought to a stand on the short stretch of 1 in 200 at Gilmerton station platform. If the majority of levers had been applied on the left hand side of the train, the platform made the releasing of the brakes a very difficult task. A stop then had to be made near Millerhill Junction, to release the wagon brakes.

One thing in the train crew's favour was that the loaded journey was always downhill, but even taking the empty wagons back to the collieries could have its problems. Train crews agreed that once the Danderhall road bridge had been reached, they knew that they would make it the rest of the way. If not, there was no alternative but to call for assistance. After the opening of Millerhill Yard, this process was speeded up, when locomotives were much closer to hand. Under the Working Instructions, the assisting engine did not couple up to the train, and had to assist all the way to Loanhead, before it could return. The standard load at this period was 45 empties and 36 loaded unfitted mineral wagons. If the empties were for the south connection to the Ramsey, drivers knew that, if they stopped opposite a particular gravestone which was visible above the wall of Loanhead cemetery, the rear of their train would be clear of the points. As the gravestone was topped with an urn, it was known as the 'Scottish Cup', reflecting the Scottish passion for football.

Over the years, there were numerous cases of trains running away, and a spectacular example of the results of 800 tons running away on the 1 in 55 gradient can been seen in the photographs. After the track alterations had been completed in respect of the formation of Millerhill Yard, runaways were diverted into the sand drag but, before this, the signalman had to let the train run onto the main line if it was clear, or allow it to pile up in the bay platform.

This method of working carried on even into the diesel era, and was changed only by the introduction of continuously-braked hopper wagons in the late 1960s.

Early Days

Between 6th November, 1873 and 23rd July, 1874, Waddell, the contractor, provided locomotive power, working traffic to and from Millerhill Junction where the NBR took over. Empties were left by the 7.00 am Portobello to Falahill, while loaded wagons had to be at Millerhill ready for picking up at 4.40 pm by a return Falahill-Leith Walk working, which dropped them off at Portobello Yard. The Shotts Iron Co.'s wagons were taken on to Shotts at 5.10 am from Portobello Yard, which also brought empties back on the return journey.

The new timetable brought into effect from 23rd July, 1874 shows one 'goods and mineral' train only each way daily, leaving Portobello at 11.25 am and returning from Roslin at 2.00 pm. This was worked by the St Leonards branch engine and guard.

As various pits and industries developed, an early morning service, starting at 7.40 am from Millerhill, appeared in the 1875 timetable. It was allowed 31 minutes to shunt at Ramsey Colliery before arriving at Loanhead at 8.41 am to shunt clear of the first down passenger to Edinburgh. If it appeared that the goods would be late in leaving Millerhill Junction, the locomotive had to run light engine to Loanhead with the Train Staff. Roslin was reached at 8.50, where 10 minutes were allowed for shunting. Traffic from Burghlee and Ramsey collieries was collected on the return journey, arriving at Portobello at 10.45 am.

The other train was retimed to leave Portobello at 12.15 pm and it too had to shunt at Loanhead, this time to allow both up and down passenger trains to pass. After shunting and weighing Ramsey Colliery traffic it proceeded to Roslin, arriving at 2.50 pm. The return trip, calling only at Loanhead to pick up the wagons weighed on the up journey, was made at 3.05 pm, reaching Millerhill at 4.16 and Portobello at 4.45 pm.

By the early 1880s, the shale oil traffic from Straiton was being worked to Whifflet, near Coatbridge, on the Caledonian Railway. The empty tank wagons were left at Straiton Sidings by the first goods train at 8.20 am, to be collected by the Clippins Oil Company 'pug'. Full tanks were uplifted at 1.00 pm by the down goods, which ran only as far as Millerhill. Their ultimate destination was the Clippins Oil Company's works at Linwood, near Paisley.

In common with the majority of British railway companies in the 19th century, the NBR favoured the 0-6-0 tender locomotive for goods services. Up to 1921, the NBR built a total of 674 0-6-0s, culminating in the 'S' class introduced 1914 (later 'J37') which lasted beyond the end of steam on the branch.

The first definite record of goods train working is to be found in the traffic census which the NBR carried out on Thursday 20th October, 1898. Details were noted of all trains worked that day on the entire system, a huge undertaking which, significantly, was not repeated.

Four trips are shown, one with No. 568, a class 'D' 0-6-0 (later class 'J33'), and the remainder in charge of No. 688, a class 'C' 0-6-0 ('J36'). No. 688 was one of the longer lived 'J36s', withdrawn in July 1959 when 67 years old, as No. 65259.

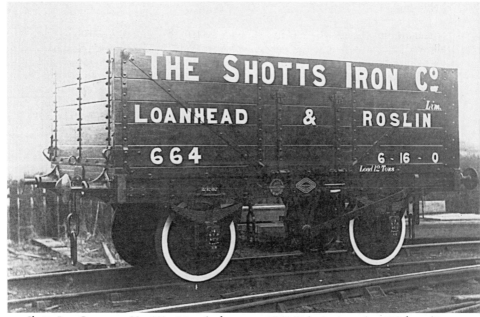

Shotts Iron Co. wagon No. 664, pictured when new at R.Y. Pickering's works at Wishaw. It was built in 1902, and had a capacity of 12 tons.   *Historical Model Railway Society*

In the mid-1930s 'J36' class 0-6-0 No. 9788 was the regular branch engine. She is pictured between trips at Portobello Yard.   *G.N. Heathcote*

LNER

The branch was classified '6' in the LNER system, introduced in 1928, which allowed locomotives up to the weight and capacity of 'J38' 0-6-0s. This class had been introduced in 1926, as a smaller-wheeled mineral traffic version of the LNER standard 'J39' 0-6-0, introduced also in 1926 and which was to be used throughout the system. In the event, the entire class of 35 engines was allocated to Scotland, remaining intact as a class until December 1962. They did not appear regularly on the branch until the later years of steam, when they replaced the 'J37s'. No. 65929, a regular on the line in 1964, was one of the last two LNER working locomotives on British Railways when withdrawn in April 1967.

In the 1930s, 'J36s' were the usual choice, including some passenger turns, using those locomotives which were dual fitted (air and vacuum brakes). Introduced in 1888, some of the class outlived their much newer counterparts, two lasting until 1967, with one (No. 673 *Maude* of 1891) preserved by the Scottish Preservation Society at Bo'ness. No. 9788 is recorded as the usual branch engine during the later 1930s.

British Railways

The 1949 BR Working Timetable, shows the service as 'suspended'. The only train is to be found under 'Control Order Engines', where No. G10 worked the 8.45 am Portobello to Glencorse, calling at all stations. Traffic, including coal from Roslin Colliery to Ramsey washer, is on an 'as required' basis.

By the mid-1950s local goods and mineral services had been grouped together in the bi-annual BR 'Train, Trip and Shunting Engine Notice'. This was to make any alterations easier to carry out, if required by changes in local circumstances. Such alterations were published monthly.

The earliest available Trip Notice in the Author's possession is for the period commencing June 1956, and shows two diagrams. The former LMS depot at Seafield, taken over by the LNER during World War II, provided the locomotives.

One, No. 149 with a 'J35' rostered to leave Portobello at 8.30 am, worked 'all stations on the Glencorse branch as required by Control'. Diagram 184 handled all of the coal traffic on a three shift, 24 hour basis, using 'B1' locomotives. Two trips each were made to Burghlee and Gilmerton collieries, while the Ramsey had three. There was a steady transfer of coal from both Roslin and Burghlee to the Ramsey washer, and empties in the opposite direction, resulting in trips between these points. At 11.55 am, a trip was made from Millerhill to Meadows Yard (between Portobello and Seafield), enabling the crew to run light engine to Seafield for a fresh locomotive. On returning to Millerhill, another light engine run was necessary to Hardengreen, south of Eskbank, this time to change crews. The second crew change was also at Hardengreen, around midnight. After the second visit to Gilmerton Colliery leaving at 4.00 am for Millerhill, the shift finished at 6.25 am back at Hardengreen, except for Monday mornings, when the engine returned to St Margaret's for weekly maintenance.

Fireman David Cairns (*left*) and his driver pose for the camera at Millerhill, before working a train of empties for Loanhead on Christmas Day, 1948. 'J35' class 0-6-0 No. 64532 carries the early 'British Railways' lettering.   *David Cairns*

Caught by one of the passengers on board the 1951 *Glen Falloch* special as it passes Loanhead box, an unidentified 0-6-0 waits in the Ramsey Colliery loop; 28th April, 1951.

Ron Glendinning

The crew of 'J37' class 0-6-0 No. 64606 will be relieved to have reached the A68 road bridge, considering the amount of leaking steam visible in this undated view, taken in the late 1950s.
J.G.Kerr, Collection Don Rowland

On an overcast Saturday in 1958, the empty stock of an excursion arrives at Loanhead double-headed by 'J37' and 'J39' class 0-6-0s.
Stewart Sellar

The 184 diagram remained unchanged apart from renumbering as E84, until 1959, when the third shift was dispensed with, and the trip did not run on Saturday afternoons or Sundays. The second shift crew travelled from Seafield to Millerhill by BR road transport.

In 1957, the 149 trip had been re-numbered E72, with a dedicated timetable, making a trip to Glencorse at 11.30 am and calling at Straiton Sidings on the return, at 12.30 pm. With the rundown of the line beyond Roslin, by 1959 E72, now 'J37'-powered, spent the period between 10.15 am and 1.35 pm working to the instructions of the Loanhead station master.

From January 1962, the E84 turn was joined by two new turns, both using class 'J37s'. E86 at 6.30 am, and E96 at 2.25 pm. The 'B1' locomotives allocated to turn E84 saw the most intensive use, with four individual trips to Bilston Glen and two to Roslin, calling at Bilston Glen on the return journey. Under the BR General Instruction dated 25th November, 1961, trains were allowed to proceed without the token to Burghlee or Bilston Glen.

The Trip Notice for April 1964, the last year of steam working, shows eight runs to Bilston Glen, two to Roslin Colliery and one to Burghlee. Two of the E58 diagrams ran through to Slateford, all of the others terminating at Millerhill Yard. The building of a connection between the Suburban Circle line and the former LMS line to Carstairs and Glasgow, which was opened on 15th March, 1959, had drastically reduced the distance travelled by coal traffic for destinations in the West of Scotland. Prior to this, all traffic from the Lothian coalfield had to be worked down to Granton Square via Easter Road and Trinity Junction, and then pushed all the way back uphill again on the ex-LMS Granton branch to Crew Junction. In addition, a toll for each wagon axle passing over

'J37' class 0-6-0 No. 64624 passes Loanhead on 21st October, 1963, with the up home signal silhouetted against the sky.   *W.A.C. Smith*

the connection at Granton Square had to be paid to the Duke of Buccleuch, under a long-standing agreement.

Any goods or local coal merchant's traffic for Loanhead was handled by the only 'J38' diagram (E58), arriving at 7.55 am. Wagons to be detached were marshalled at the rear of the train, to simplify shunting.

Dieselisation

For the engine crews, the introduction of diesel power to the branch in the spring of 1964 could not have been more dramatic. They were able to swap the often cold and dirty steam engine cab for the comfort of a Clayton 900 hp Type '1' (later class '17'). These locomotives had been introduced in 1962, to fill the gap between the 350 hp shunters (later class '08') which were suitable only for short trips, and the larger horsepower classes. Powered by two Paxman 450 hp engines giving 40,000 lb. of tractive effort, they appeared eminently suitable for branch line work. Their spacious cabs were located centrally, giving an excellent view in both directions, while the specification included a hotplate for the use of the crew. The guards' working conditions remained unchanged, however, as loose coupled wagons were still in use.

To reduce light engine movements between Millerhill and Haymarket Shed a new refuelling depot had been built within the yard complex, with a train crew signing-on point. Locomotives returned to Haymarket depot once a week for maintenance.

The 1967 Trip Notice shows a daily service of 10 trains, with three diagrams, two of them double-shifted, using 900 hp diesel locomotives, as the Claytons were officially referred to. The first train of the day ran to Roslin Colliery, arriving at 6.25 am, and called at Bilston Glen on the return journey. All other trips served Bilston Glen, the last run leaving at 8.55 pm. The scrap metal output from the site of Gilmerton Colliery was catered for by the 6.45 am ex-Millerhill, although with only 15 minutes allowed for shunting the traffic must have been light.

During the late 1960s, it became clear that the Claytons were not up to some of the duties expected of them, as if worked hard they had a tendency to catch fire, resulting in an alarming eruption of flames from their exhausts which were located centrally in each windscreen. All had disappeared by the early 1970s, leaving the branch trains in the charge of class '20' and '26' locomotives.

The class '20s' were found usually in pairs, nose to nose, to improve enginemen's visibility, and powered the occasional fitted coal train. These were easily identified by the wagon livery of bauxite, rather than the grey of the unfitted mineral wagons.

By 1969, the advent of the 'Merry-go-Round' (MGR) service to Cockenzie power station was a major new source of traffic, which was to last for the next 20 years. The existing class '26' locomotives were used, several being modified to enable them to maintain the required 0.5 mph when unloading at Cockenzie. Standard rakes of 29, 32 tonne air braked hopper wagons were used, increasing the capacity of each train to 928 tonnes.

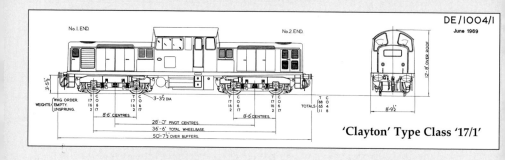

DE/1004/1
June 1969

'Clayton' Type Class '17/1'

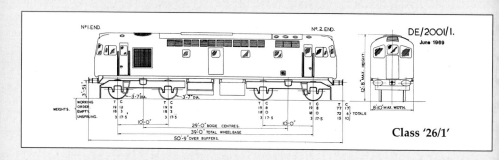

DE/2001/1.
June 1969

Class '26/1'

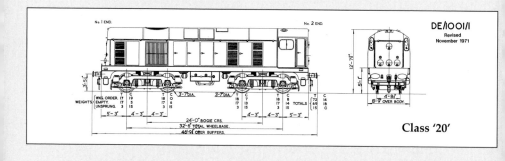

DE/1001/1
Revised
November 1971

Class '20'

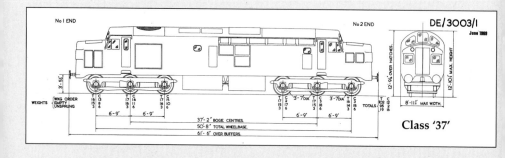

DE/3003/1
June 1969

Class '37'

In July 1964 a 'Clayton' pauses for instructions from the Loanhead signalman, with the afternoon E84 trip to Roslin Colliery. *Author*

The evening sun catches 'Clayton' No. D8556 passing Gilmerton with a down train in September 1964. *Author*

Making a welcome change from the usual train of MGR hoppers, a class '26' approaches Gilmerton in the summer of 1978 with 16 ton open wagons. The distinctive shape of the Ramsey washer is visible on the skyline, above the locomotive. Note the express train headlamp code!
Bill Roberton

Above: Class '26' No. 26 006 appears to be recently 'ex-works' in BR 'large logo' livery when caught approaching Bilston Glen Colliery sidings on 1st March, 1988. At this period 'yard working' commenced at the notice board to the right of the signal post. *Dr M. Rhodes*

Left: Class '26s' were used to clear Bilston Glen site, in this case blue liveried No. 26 021 approaches Millerhill on the last day of February 1991. *Max Fowler*

By February 1991, the task of removing the stockpiled coal from Bilston Glen had almost been completed. On the 28th of the month, class '37' No. 37080 brings another 25 hoppers past Edgefield road bridge, through the ever increasing piles of litter.   *Bill Roberton*

No. 37 080 stands at the loading point, before returning to Cockenzie Power Station on 28th March, 1991.   *Bill Roberton*

Designated 'HOP AB' by BR, this 32-tonne hopper pictured at Millerhill on 12th June, 1967 is in original condition. Many of these vehicles reverted to this configuration after the removal of overhead bunker loading systems from collieries in the 1980s. No. B350165 was built at British Railways' Shildon works in 1965.   *Don Rowland*

The addition of hoods, which reduced dust and loss during transit, altered the appearance of these wagons considerably, as shown in this shot of B51115, again at Millerhill. The tare weight was increased from 13.7t to 14t; 14th April, 1969.   *Don Rowland*

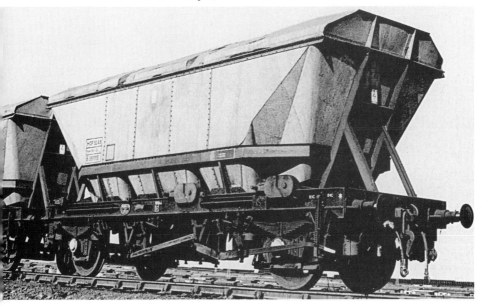

Class '26' No. 26 006 brings train 7B09 (the first of the day) past the site of Straiton Sidings, during the removal of the coal stocks from Bilston Glen Colliery. The grain silos of Alexander Inglis & Sons and the tower of the United Free Church form the skyline; 2nd May, 1991.

Dr M. Rhodes

On the 2nd May, 1991, class '26' No. 26 006 waits amid the desolation following the demolition of Bilston Glen Colliery for the hopper wagons to be loaded from the last of the stockpile.

Dr M. Rhodes

By 1996, the practice of using a main line locomotive to shunt Monktonhall Colliery had been replaced by a class '08' shunter from the Transrail Millerhill depot. *Carlo Rubino*

This view from the overbridge at Millerhill shows the branch connection on the left, with the line to the former East Coast Electrification Depot straight ahead. Class '56' No. 56 129 is flagged over the new road leading to the former BR locomotive maintenance depot. *Carlo Rubino*

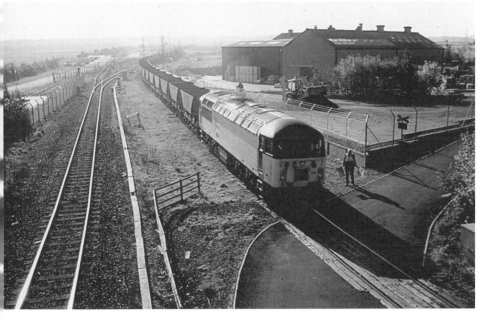

After the long Miners' strike of 1984-5 had been resolved, it was some time before a full train service could resume, as the HAA hopper wagons, which had lain almost unused during the strike period, had to be made ready for traffic. The first train was observed on 8th March, 1985, hauled by class '26' No. 26 001. Such was the demand for empty wagons that the service was extended to Sundays for a period, and the unusual sight of three class '26' locomotives coupled together (Nos. 26 006, 26 004, and 26 014) was observed passing Loanhead for Millerhill, at 2.45 pm on Monday 18th March. Over the next two years almost any form of motive power could be seen, from class '20s', through classes '26' and '27', up to class '37'. Even class '25' locomotives appeared infrequently, with No. 25 240 observed propelling a brake van back to Millerhill. The date of this sighting is, unfortunately, not recorded. Double-heading was frequent, occasionally with one locomotive at each end, plus light engine movements due to unbalanced workings.

Once a year, usually in June, the continuing monotony of coal trains was relieved by the appearance of the weed killing train, in charge of a class '26', its coaches prompting enquiries by the townspeople of Loanhead about the re-introduction of a passenger service! No. 26 024 was in charge on 10th June, 1988, seen passing the site of Loanhead station at 12.10 pm, in the up direction.

When the regular shunters at Bilston Glen were both under repair, a replacement was hired from BR, usually towed by a main line locomotive, but class '08' No. 08 570 made the journey from Millerhill unaided on 16th August, 1985. On 1st March, 1988, 08 570 was photographed at the colliery, and was observed returning to Millerhill, towed by a class '20', on the 9th of that month.

After the closure of Bilston Glen in 1989, the remaining stockpiles of coal took several years to clear, as mentioned earlier. Towards the end of this operation, the mechanised loading facilities had been demolished, and mechanical shovels had to be brought in to load the hopper wagons. The hoods had to be removed from the wagons to allow for this change in loading arrangements, thus reverting to their original appearance, before their employment in MGR service.

Until May 1997, the stub of the branch was still in use, to enable locomotives to run round trains for Monktonhall Colliery. They had to pass the branch down home signal (No. M3), to release the interlocking. Before privatisation, this resulted in class '56' locomotives standing in deep undergrowth while waiting for the road, reminiscent of little used branch lines of the past. Latterly, a class '08' shunter was to be found shunting the colliery sidings, based at the former BR Millerhill depot, now owned by English, Welsh and Scottish Railways.

Chapter Twelve

Signalling

During the lifetime of the branch, four major re-signalling programmes have been undertaken, ironically, the most recent within a year of the cessation of traffic. From the earliest interlocking installation and semaphore signals to the latest Track Circuit Block, axle counters and motorised points, each has reflected the latest technology of the day.

By the time the line opened, the signalling of railways had become relatively sophisticated, and in essentials not greatly different from the standards of today. The electric telegraph, in one form or another, had been around for many years as a simple means of communication. Its derivative, the 'block telegraph' system of train control, was a more recent development that was rapidly gaining ground.

The interlocking of points and signals was also, by that time, recognised as a necessity, and the 'elevated signal box' which housed the signalman and his levers was becoming an ever more common sight on the railway.

There were several specialist contractors who could offer efficient apparatus for both block working and interlocking. On the ELR Messrs Stevens & Sons of Glasgow (whose equipment was used by all the railway companies of Scotland except for the Highland Railway) provided the signals and the interlocking; the telegraph instruments used on the branch were supplied by Tyer & Co. of London.

The new junction with the main line and the signal box at Millerhill were inspected by Lt Col Hutchinson on behalf of the Board of Trade on 1st October, 1873. He was able to report that 'an excellent cabin had been constructed with levers for working the points and signals interlocked with one another'. One more signal was to be added and a portion of the sidings was to be completed. He noted that the station and passenger arrangements at the station would have to be inspected, when notice was given for the opening of the ELR to passenger traffic. He required locking bars to be fitted to all points over which passenger trains would pass. The signal box was formally opened on 6th November, 1873.

The ELR itself was inspected for suitability for passenger train working on 22nd July, 1874 but, unfortunately, the report makes little detailed reference to the signalling (very much a feature of Board of Trade reports at that time). The inspecting officer noted that the points and signals on the line were interlocked but required locking bars to be fitted to points to prevent them moving under the trains. He also required that 'the combined system of block telegraph and train staff' working should be adopted.

Under this system (applicable only to single lines) a train had to be properly signalled between 'block posts' by the block telegraph and, as an extra measure of security, carry a wooden or metal 'train staff' which gave exclusive rights to occupy the 'block section' between two block posts. If two separate trains wished to run after each other in the same direction, a ticket was made out to authorise the driver of the first train to proceed through the block section and the train staff (which had to be shown to him) would follow. The block telegraph instruments would indicate when the train had arrived safe and

Millerhill Junction signal box, pictured in 1962, shortly before it was replaced by the new power box, as part of the marshalling yard alterations. *Signalling Record Society*

The interior of Millerhill Junction box, showing the track diagram, instrument shelf and lever frame. *Signalling Record Society*

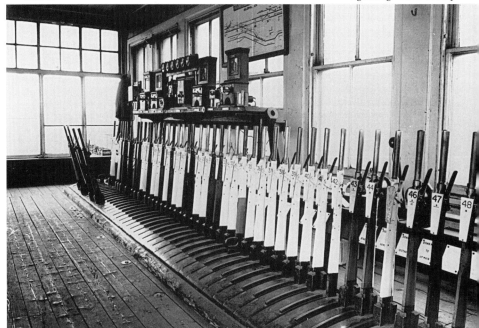

complete, and the second train could then be signalled to follow, carrying the train staff.

It is a curiosity that, despite the recommendation of the inspecting officer, the block telegraph does not appear to have been installed on this, first, part of the railway. The statutory returns from the railway company to the Board of Trade in 1877 (required under the Regulation of Railways Act of 1873), and the Appendix to the Working Timetable of 1st June, 1882, give the working of the line as 'Method 2 - Working by Train Staff' with Loanhead and Millerhill as the adjacent staff stations. Although 'train tickets' are to be used, the working is not that of Method 3 - 'Working under combined systems of Block Telegraph and Train Staff and Ticket'.

The train staffs were each numbered and of a different colour, to ease identification. The Millerhill to Loanhead staff was No. 0 and coloured red, and that for Loanhead to Roslin was No. 2 and coloured white. The staff provided in 1877 for the extension to Glencorse was coloured dark blue.

No plans have survived showing the signalling of the branch as a whole, but a plan of the signalling at Gilmerton survives in the Scottish Record Office (SRO). This plan is dated 7th September, 1874, i.e. after the inspection, so it may be reasonable to assume that it was prepared to show the arrangement subsequent to the adoption of the Board of Trade requirements. A facing point lock had been fitted and the fact that it was worked by a lever at the end of the frame suggests that it was an afterthought (there are other contemporary examples to corroborate the practice). Curiously, there are no safety points in the sidings and, even more curiously, no requirement to fit them!

Though Gilmerton was never a block post it was fitted up with signals and properly interlocked, as were all the other signal boxes whether block posts or not. A similar situation arose at the new Straiton Sidings where a new signal box (not a block post) was provided in 1877 to control points and signals for new sidings.

From all the evidence to hand we can deduce that when the line opened there were signal boxes at Millerhill Junction (block post), Gilmerton (non block post), Loanhead (block post), Burghlee (non block post) and Roslin (block post). The 1877 extension brought new boxes to the Glasgow Ironworks Junction, for Roslin Colliery (non block post) and Glencorse (block post).

Some letters from Stevens & Sons, New City Road, Glasgow, to Thomas Bouch, Engineer, ELR have survived in the SRO:

29th January, 1877

We are in receipt of your favour of 26th ult. and beg to inform you that lock apparatus lot of material will be forwarded tomorrow, Tuesday, the signals to follow on Friday, and then the men will follow to fix them.

27th February, 1877

Pass requested for three men between Edinburgh and Roslin. Pass No. 104 was returned on July 12th.

2nd April, 1877

Our Mr Deakin will go on the ELR tomorrow to see the site of the proposed cabin for the Glasgow Iron Co.'s branch, leaving by the 8 am train. Will you kindly renew enclosed pass.

Signalman Tom Simcock stands outside his box in 1961. At some stage the upper storey of the original all-brick structure has been replaced and extended, to provide an improved view. Note the NBR shunt signal in the foreground, and the BR wooden-bodied coal wagon in the Ramsey Colliery sidings, even at this late date. *Mike Smith*

Loanhead box, on 18th October, 1971, shortly before closure. The tall fence surrounding the site of the former Ramsey Colliery can be seen to the left. The brick-built relay room would remain after demolition of the box. *Ken Falconer*

1st August, 1877
Will you please appoint a day next week for one of your assistants to meet ours to measure the work done on the ELR, and oblige.

Lt Col Hutchinson inspected the new extension on 16th May, 1877 and made the following comments in his report:

At Roslin (18 levers) an Up starting signal was necessary, the facing points leading to the engine shed were to be removed and placed in the goods loop, and No. 12 lever should lock No. 4 lever.

Immediately south of Roslin station, there was a junction to serve the Glasgow Iron Co.'s new sidings to serve Roslin Colliery, which was situated on a gradient of 1 in 66 falling towards Roslin goods yard, from which it was 300 yards distant. It was provided with its own cabin, which was new. He asked if it might not be better in a way to continue the mineral line up to an overbridge about 80 yards from the goods yard points, and then lay parallel rails through the bridge to join the engine shed sidings. If this was not done a satisfactory arrangement would have to be made so as to ensure that the goods yard points were locked open for the goods yard when any up train was stopping to work the siding junction.

At Glencorse (14 levers) there were new sidings and a new signal cabin. There were several alterations required here:

Nos. 1 and 5 levers were to interlock;
Nos. 1 and 6 signal arms were to be interchanged and No. 6 cut shorter and placed lower on the post;
Nos. 5 and 8 levers were not to interlock;
The position of No. 12 points was to be reversed so as to lie open to the goods yard and to be locked in that position by the lowering of No. 3 signal.

As there was a possibility of extending the line to Penicuik, Hutchinson suggested that the turntable presently at Roslin might be more use if shifted to Glencorse. He required an undertaking from the company that no engines would run tender first from Roslin to Edinburgh, and a further undertaking that the mode of working the new extension would be Absolute Block Telegraph with Train Staff. On 26th June he re-inspected the line and found that his requirements had been complied with. In the case of the means that had been provided for ensuring that the goods yard points at Roslin were locked open when a train was shunting at the Glasgow Iron Co.'s siding (Roslin Colliery, also known as the Moat Pit), the two keys were to be rivetted together and not connected by a chain. This was to be attended to at once.

Not mentioned by Hutchinson was the work undertaken in Glencorse signal box to meet his requirements. The 14 existing levers in the locking frame were at 5¼ in. centres and three extra levers had had to be added; as space between the end of the frame and the wall of the signal box was restricted, the new levers were installed at 4¼ in. centres.

Sometime between 1891 and 1898 (actual date uncertain), the old Train Staff working (without block telegraph) was discontinued between Millerhill and Roslin and replaced by the Tyer's Electric Train Tablet system. The instruments employed

The fireman of this 'J37' class 0-6-0 reaches for the Loanhead-Millerhill token, held by signalman Tom Simcock, in June 1961. *Mike Smith*

The Loanhead-Eastfield Siding train staff, dating from the 1900s.
Author, courtesy Forbes Alexander

were of the No. 1 type that required a tablet, once withdrawn from an instrument, to be taken through the section and placed in the instrument at the next token point, before another could be obtained for a movement in either direction.

With adoption of the tablet system it was no longer necessary to provide signals to protect the points of intermediate sidings; the tablet could be used to unlock a ground-mounted frame of small levers which would control the siding points and their facing point lock. Once the levers were released, the tablet would remain locked in the ground frame until the levers were replaced in their normal position.

The signal boxes at Straiton, Edgefield and Burghlee were closed around the turn of the century, and their points were thereafter worked by the ground frames controlled by tablet lock. Gilmerton box appears to have been retained, possibly due to the combination of the goods yard and Gilmerton Colliery traffic.

The section from Roslin to Glencorse continued to be operated by Train Staff with Absolute Block until some time no later than 1907, when 'converted' tablet instruments were provided throughout the entire branch. These instruments were of the original No. 1 type which had been converted (extensively) to allow a tablet, once withdrawn, to be replaced in its own instrument without being taken through the section. This feature was useful if a train was cancelled, or if a train was required to work an intermediate siding without continuing on through the block section but returning to the signal box which had issued the tablet.

At some time before 1930 the signal box at Loanhead, which had had a 16-lever frame, was substantially reconstructed to accommodate a 30-lever frame to work the points and signals added when the coal washer was installed at the Ramsey Colliery. Two new connections were made to the main line, one immediately north of the box, and another at the south end of the station. A headshunt was also added to the goods yard layout. This 'new' frame was to Stevens Old Pattern and was made up from spare parts. Nominally described as a frame with levers at 4¼ in. centres, between levers 10 and 21 the levers were actually at 5¼ in. centres.

The withdrawal of the passenger train service led inevitably to economies in the signalling. Glencorse and Roslin boxes closed on 25th March, 1934, and ground frames were substituted to work the main line points. The electric tablet was removed south of Loanhead and 'One Engine in Steam' working with train staff was introduced between Loanhead and the end of the branch. To protect the main line at Glencorse from possible runaways from the mineral extension, the

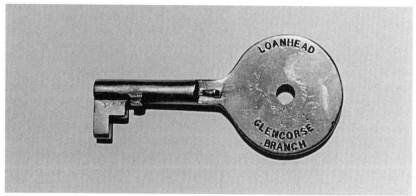

The Annett's key for the Loanhead-Glencorse section, used in the British Railways era.
Author, courtesy Rae Montgomery

points were normally left open for the goods yard, and the up starting signal was retained to warn drivers of this fact. This was the only remaining semaphore signal south of Loanhead, surviving until closure of the station in 1959.

These arrangements were to remain in place until 1961, when alterations became necessary at Loanhead to handle traffic from Bilston Glen Colliery. The goods yard headshunt was extended northwards to form a new loop, signalled in both directions. All the remaining Stevens pattern signal arms were removed and replaced with standard upper-quadrant arms, and several new tubular posts appeared to replace some of the old lattice ones.

At the junction with the colliery (about 750 yards south of the signal box) two separate motor-operated connections were installed, for incoming and outgoing traffic. Four new signals, also motor operated, were also provided, numbered 31 to 16. A small switch panel in Loanhead box controlled the new layout. The new down outer home signal (No. 27), which protected the new junction from the Roslin direction, remained mechanically worked. The entire layout was track circuited, with the odd exception of the new loop.

Further changes came one year later with the opening of Millerhill Yard on 6th May, 1962, when the original junction box of 1873 was abolished and replaced by a new power box, also called Millerhill, as explained in Chapter Eight. The electric tablet was removed from the Millerhill-Loanhead section, and the line was track circuited throughout. Lever No. 1 at Loanhead, which formerly worked the up distant signal, became the 'acceptance lever', which, when reversed, gave permission for Millerhill to clear the colour-light signals leading to Loanhead. Another function of this lever was to release the ground frame at Gilmerton Colliery, for up direction movements.

After the closure of Roslin Colliery in 1969, and the withdrawal of goods facilities, the need for a signal box at Loanhead declined, and rationalisation of the layout led to the closure of the box on 18th June, 1972. Control of the branch to Bilston Glen passed to Millerhill power box. Track Circuit Block working was abolished and 'One Train Working' by telephone substituted. At the

Bilston Glen junction the remains of the branch beyond the ingoing connection were removed, and the former outgoing connection, with its two signals, was converted to mechanical operation from a new 5-lever ground frame. A telephone connection to Millerhill was provided. Vandalism of this installation became a recurring problem, and the signals were eventually abandoned.

New semaphore signals made an unexpected return to the branch on 16th October, 1988, in connection with the bridgeworks near the site of Straiton Sidings for the new Edinburgh City Bypass (A720). A new 3-lever ground frame was provided immediately on the south side of the site of the work, on the left of drivers of down trains. In both directions, there were semaphore stop signals 190 yards from the site, on the left of drivers, with the arms 18 feet above rail level. Reflectorised distant boards, with AWS track equipment, were provided approximately 1,800 yards in each direction. During the period of possession, the Person In Charge Of the Possession (PICOP) was responsible for the operation of the signals. Outwith the period of possession, the signals were normally in the 'clear' position, locked by No. 2 lever, which was itself locked by a padlock, the key to which was retained by the PICOP.

On 6th December, 1988 the life-expired signalling at Millerhill was replaced by a new box operating a much reduced and simplified layout. Track Circuit Block working was re-installed on the branch, using axle counters. The ground frame and semaphores at Bilston Glen were removed and a two aspect (red/green) colour light signal (M1) was erected to control movements onto the single line.

After closure of Bilston Glen in 1989, the branch remained open for a further two years while the coal stocks were removed, after which the line was put out of use from the Kaim road overbridge (No. 2). The branch home signal M3 was retained for use by locomotives serving Monktonhall Colliery, until closure of the latter in 1997.

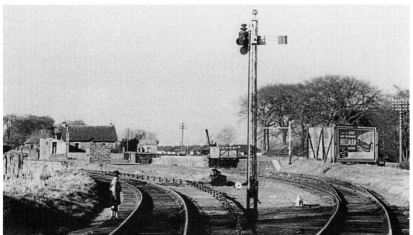

Taken on 17th April, 1955, this view of Glencorse (*looking north*) shows the one remaining signal and the relevant ground frame left after the alterations of 1934. Note the solitary wagon in the goods yard and the advertisement for Hillman cars.   *J.L. Stevenson*

Chapter Thirteen

Accidents

During the lifetime of the line, there has been no recorded instance of any passenger fatalities. Regrettably, the same cannot be said for railway company employees and trespassers. As explained in Chapter Two, the railway department of the Board of Trade had to be informed of all railway accidents involving personal injury, however trivial. Over the years the inspecting officers' reports repeatedly warned of the dangers to employees involved in shunting and marshalling trains, in an effort to reduce the large number of injuries sustained by railwaymen.

While, strictly speaking not occurring on ELR property, as early as October 1874 George Horsburgh, a clerk of the Shotts Iron Co., sustained a leg injury as a result of setting some wagons in motion at Ramsey Colliery. The dangers associated with the coming of the railway were evidently still to be appreciated by the local population.

Less than two years later, the first fatality occurred near Roslin, when a trespasser was run over by a passenger train on 14th April, 1876. No further details are recorded, reflecting the attitude of the time to those who chose to ignore the warning signs which gave the maximum fine of 'forty shillings', a large sum in those days.

No further instances are recorded until 21st April, 1911, when goods guard Marr had a lucky escape on the afternoon Millerhill-Glencorse mineral train. Approaching the stone overbridge north of Gilmerton, he heard a rattling noise coming from underneath the brake van. Thinking that some part of the brake rigging had broken loose, he hurriedly went out onto the footboard, and was stooping down to inspect the brake gearing when he came into contact with the stone abutment of the bridge, and fell onto the ballast. His only injury was a bruised hip, and the report states that he insisted on completing his inspection of the brake gearing and found it to be in order. He was only 1 hour 37 minutes into his 10 hour shift, and, no doubt would have carried on working until his allotted time. The BoT inspector recorded a verdict of misadventure.

Tragedy struck just over a year later, when the 7.52 pm from Glencorse came to grief between Roslin and Loanhead, the unfortunate fireman losing his life. Tuesday 2nd July, 1912 was a fine dry evening as the train, hauled by 'R' class 4-4-0T No. 104 running bunker first, left Roslin at 7.56 pm. It consisted of four 6-wheel coaches, a 3rd class brake, a 3rd class coach, 1st class coach and another 3rd class brake bringing up the rear. The driver, James McArthur from Penicuik, had 22 years' service with the NBR, while his fireman, 21-year old John Stewart of Roslin, had been branch fireman for one year. Alexander Hutchinson, the guard, had the longest service, 28 years as a guard, out of a total of 39 with the company.

Approximately 1,700 yards north of Roslin station, the train became derailed on the outside of a right-hand curve and, after travelling upright for some distance, the locomotive struck the left side of a cutting. The fireman was thrown out of the right-hand side of the cab and crushed, as the engine toppled over on to its right-hand side, ending up at right-angles to the track, jammed between the sides of the cutting. The driver managed to remain on the engine, and was badly shaken and bruised. Of the dozen or so passengers, only three were slightly injured. Although suffering from shock, McArthur searched for his mate, but found him to be dead, his body trapped beneath the locomotive. He also found the engine bogie under the leading end of the second coach, which led to speculation that an axle or the pivot pin had sheared. Hutchinson, assisted by two male passengers, helped the rest of the occupants out of the carriages, which were derailed but upright, with the exception of the first, which had been separated from the rest and was leaning to the right, against the locomotive. One of the passengers, a Mrs Watkins of Penicuik, who was travelling to Loanhead with her four-year-old daughter, was so shocked that she ran to the Edinburgh road and caught the motor bus back to Penicuik, without waiting for assistance.

News of the accident spread rapidly through the district, and the breakdown gang was summoned from St Margaret's, while Mr Boath, the district engineer arrived by taxi to take charge of operations. It took several hours to raise the engine sufficently to remove the body, this being achieved by 11 pm. A stretcher party from the Loanhead Territorials, led by Sergeant Smith, who had arrived to assist, then removed the fireman's body to Roslin, to the house of his father, who was a workman in the gunpowder mills. A number of county policemen had to be summoned, to control the large crowd which had gathered. It appears that this particular service was known locally as the 'golfers' train', being used by players returning to Edinburgh, but none were present that day, due to the uncertain weather.

After No. 104 had been re-railed, it was taken, minus its bogie, to the nearest siding at Burghlee Colliery, where the bogie was refitted. All of the wheels were checked and found to conform to the track guage.

The BoT inquiry was held the following Saturday in Edinburgh, by Major Pringle, and his report gives an insight into railway working of the period.

Before recounting the statements of the various witnesses and company officials, Major Pringle described the condition of the line at the point of the accident, which had occurred on a gradually falling gradient. The track had been relaid in 1911, using old 24 ft-long ex-main line rails, manufactured in 1888, which had weighed 84 lb./yard, but now weighed 79 lb./yard. Re-sleepering with 10 sleepers to each rail length and 40 lb. chairs had been carried out earlier in the year, up to a point near to the first point of derailment, the remainder being nine sleepers per length and 35 lb.chairs. The ash ballast was described as 'light' and 'somewhat deficient in quantity', but the inspector thought the permanent way 'in fair condition', and 'adequate 'for the traffic.

Evidence was heard from various railway company employees, starting with the two signalmen, Walter Irving at Roslin and Farquhar Gunn at Loanhead. They had both booked on at 5 pm for a 12 hour shift, and stated that the normal time taken for a train to travel between Roslin and Loanhead varied between 3 and 4½ minutes.

Guard Hutchinson then gave his statement. He had come on duty at 11 am, and would normally have finished at 9.35 pm, and had spoken to the driver at

Glencorse and saw nothing unusual in his manner. They had left Roslin at 7.56 pm by his watch, the same time as the day before, when they had taken four minutes to reach Loanhead, and he estimated their speed at between 20 and 25 miles per hour. At the point of the derailment, he was in the brake compartment of the last coach, and felt an unusual rocking motion, before he realised that his vehicle was off the road. After the van came to rest, he got out and found the train in the position described earlier. He had not been so much as thrown off his seat by the movement, and had not experienced any previous problems on this section.

Driver McArthur was interviewed next, and stated that he had been a driver for 13 years, and had spent the last 5½ of these on the branch with No. 104. On the day of the accident he had started work at 2.22 pm., usually finishing at 12.22 am. No. 104 was normally overhauled every 18 months, the last being completed on 25th May, 1912. He never had any difficulty in driving the locomotive, but had noticed that it did oscillate where the track was 'slack', at the Moat farm crossing near Roslin, for example. The locomotive was never turned, which indicates that the Roslin turntable was out of use by this period. He confirmed that the engine rode more steadily when travelling chimney first, which was to be expected with a 4-4-0T wheel arrangement. His first indication that something was wrong occured when the leading driving wheels derailed to the left, and both men were thrown about the footplate as the wheels rode over the sleepers. The fireman was thrown out as the engine turned over, despite the cab doors being closed. After realising that he could do nothing for him, McArthur checked the driving wheel springs as he thought that one had broken, but found them intact. He had driven past the spot three times in the previous two hours, and had noted nothing unusual. An empty coal train to Roslin Colliery had also used the section of track during this period.

The district locomotive superintendent, George McLaren, who had overseen the removal of the damaged train, stated that he could not find any evidence of damage to the rolling stock to show why the derailment had ocurred. He described how No. 104 had been overhauled the previous May, when the wheels were turned up, the axleboxes lined and bored and the springs reset. The cylinders, valve gear and boiler were also repaired. 'This sort of general repair work is carried out on an engine of this type, and with this amount of mileage once in 15 or 18 months. This particular engine has worked on the branch for over 30 years', he added.

It was now the turn of James Davidson the permanent way inspector, with his foreman Thomas Mercer and leading man Peter Curran to give their evidence. Davidson had walked over the section between Loanhead and Roslin a week earlier (25th June) and found it in 'good order'. He had arrived at the scene at 2.30 am and had examined the track southwards from the point that the train had come to rest. There were several marks on the rail head about 112 yards to the south, which indicated the point of the initial derailment. The track gauge was correct here, and the sleepers undisturbed. He thought that the track would be suitable for speeds up to 40 mph.

In his conclusion, Major Pringle found great difficulty in pinpointing the cause of the accident. He discounted the theory that the bogie had become detatched before the locomotive left the rails, as he calculated that the leading driving wheels would have had to be raised 4½ inches above the rails before the pivot pin could be freed. In fact, he concluded that the bogie played a major part in keeping the locomotive upright after the driving wheels left the rails. As to the condition of the track, he agreed that it was suitable for speeds up to 40 mph, but noted that when the rails were re-used on the branch they were turned end for end, resulting in the slight 'lip' which forms on the outside of the railhead now being on the inside edge.

His main concern was the actual speed of the train at the point where the locomotive left the rails, as the driver's estimate of 20 mph appeared to him to be unlikely. Steam was applied from the time of leaving Roslin, and with the line falling at 1 in 90 for the half mile to the site of the accident, and the 5 ft driving wheel diameter, he was in no doubt that the speed would have been much higher.

He was also critical of the practice of running this type of locomotive in reverse, as 'the oscillation is always greater with the the coupled wheels in this position, and is further accentuated when descending falling gradients or by any considerable speed'.

He then studied the booked timings of passenger trains, and found that the speed must exceed 40 mph in places, if trains were to keep to the timetable. Deducting a minute for platform work at each station, the average booked speed between Glencorse and Portobello was about 32 mph. The average start to stop speeds between each station were also given, as per the following table:

From	To	Distance (miles)	Average Speed
Glencorse	Roslin	2	40
Roslin	Loanhead	1.2	25
Loanhead	Gilmerton	1.5	22.5
Gilmerton	Millerhill	2.75	41.25
Millerhill	Portobello	3.25	32.5

He concluded his report thus:

> After full consideration of all available evidence, I am of opinion that the derailment was mainly due to the train running with coupled wheels leading, at a speed higher than is justifiable for safety, and possibly higher than the superelevation on the curve justified.

It would appear that the BoT had overlooked the original statement made by the ELR back in 1877, when they had declared that no locomotive would be worked tender first from Glencorse. The assumption can be made that the accident would never have occurred if the turntable had been installed at the terminus, instead of at Roslin.

The resultant damage was summarised as an appendix to the report:

Two illustrations of the aftermath of a loaded coal train running into the sand drag at Millerhill.
The remains of several 16 ton mineral wagons have been cleared from the running lines, to be
removed at a later date; November 1967.   *(Both) G.N. Turnbull*

Rolling Stock:
Engine No. 104:
Bogie frame and stay rod bent; bogie horn block broken; bogie centre broken; smokebox door and front plate damaged; left side of cab damaged; hand rails bent; left side tank cleading damaged; footplate and angle irons damaged; tallow cock broken; left piston head broken; brake shaft bent and brake gearing damaged; footstep broken; rail guards broken; injector pipes bent and tank lid broken.
Brake third No. 1145:
One coupling screw broken; one step board damaged; two step boards destroyed; three end panels destroyed; one buffer rod bent; one buffer casting broken; four step hangers destroyed;and roof slightly damaged.
Third No. 1497:
One end badly damaged; one buffer rod bent; one end step destroyed; one step board damaged and one glass broken.
First No. 12:
Top footboard damaged and two buffer rods bent.

Permanent way:
113 sleepers broken; 8 rails broken; 79 keys broken; 80 spikes broken; 13 chairs broken.

Some years later Millerhill Junction was the scene of another accident involving two goods trains on 12th January, 1917, which blocked the Waverley Route for some hours. The night goods from Carlisle to Glasgow was approaching the junction at 6 am when it collided with the 5.40 am Millerhill-Burghlee empty mineral train, which appears to have been running late. While there was a great deal of damage to wagons of both trains, some being thrown onto the platform, the only casualty was the guard of the branch train, who suffered a bruised eye. The Midland night express from London was stopped at Eskbank, and passengers for Dundee and Aberdeen taken to Edinburgh by buses hired from the Scottish Motor Traction Co. The up line had been cleared by 9.30 am. and the Polton branch train was used to convey the remaining passengers to Edinburgh from Eskbank, working 'wrong line' past the obstruction. Both lines were reopened by midday.

Working trains down the 1 in 55 to Millerhill has always required extreme care, and on several occasions the signalman has had to make the decision whether to let the train out onto the main line in the hope that it could pull up on the level, or divert it into the dock platform, with catastrophic results.

The details of two such runaways have survived, one in steam days, while the other was as late as 1967. The latter happened after the sand drag had been provided, minimising the damage.

The events of 1912 were recalled 43 years later, when another railwayman lost his life working a branch train. On 10th November, 1955, a 'J38' with 35 wagons from Burghlee was passing Gilmerton when the main steam brake pipe between the locomotive and tender fractured, rendering the brake useless. As the train gained speed, the driver decided that both he and the fireman should jump, which they did. However, while the fireman landed almost unhurt down an embankment, the line had entered a short stretch of cutting by the time the driver leapt off, and he fell to his death under the train. Ironically, the Millerhill signalman was able to set the road for the main line, and the train came to a stand near Niddrie South. It appears that BR were in the process of replacing the brake pipe on this class of locomotive with a modified version, but this particular engine had not been dealt with by the time of the accident.

As explained in Chapter Ten, while dieselisation had improved the locomen's lot, trains remained loose coupled, until the advent of air braked wagons after 1969. On 30th October, 1967 No. D8566, a 'Clayton' Type '1' locomotive left Bilston Glen at 6.04 pm with 37 loaded 16 ton mineral wagons. After a stop to pin down the wagon brakes at underbridge No. 9 (just north of the site of Straiton Sidings) the locomotive was unable to restart due to wheelslip on the damp rail. Several brakes were released, which allowed the train to get under way. These were then re-applied and the journey resumed normally as far as the Gilmerton road underbridge, where the speed increased to 15 mph. Both the engine and van brakes were fully applied but to no avail, the speed increasing to around 20 mph. In this case, the Millerhill signalman did not have the option of allowing the runaway onto the main line, as he had accepted a MGR train from Monktonhall Colliery, which locked the branch home signal (No. M27) at danger, also setting the points for the sand drag. His first intimation that anything was amiss was the ringing of the alarm bell indicating that the runaway had passed signal M27 at 6.35 pm, whereupon he sent the 'Obstruction Danger' signal to Loanhead. The train was diverted into the sand drag at between 20 and 25 miles per hour, derailing the locomotive and the first seven wagons, while the other 30 wagons and the brake van kept the rails and were undamaged.

The crew were unhurt, and the undamaged portion of the train was removed by the locomotive of train No. E27, which had been at Bilston Glen. Extraction of the wagons, piled up in two levels, and No. D8566, which was buried up to solebar level, posed a more difficult problem, as only the tool van had been sent from Haymarket Shed. It was decided that nothing could be achieved without a breakdown crane, which arrived the next day from Eastfield, Glasgow, and succeeded in clearing the wagons. No. D8566 proved beyond the capacity of the crane on its own, and had to wait another day until another crane was summoned from Polmadie, also in Glasgow. Even then it took 3½ hours to re-rail the diesel, which had suffered only minor damage.

The subsequent inquiry held the driver and guard jointly responsible, as they had not fully complied with the 'Apply Wagon Brakes' instructions, which also stated that when working the Loanhead branch by diesel locomotive the speed on falling gradients must not exceed 10 mph. From their statements, it was proved that the driver had not indicated, by sounding the engine's horn to the guard that he was satisfied with the number of wagon brakes pinned down, and nothing could be found to indicate that any of the brakes on the train were faulty. With the gradual replacement of unfitted wagons, thankfully, this type of accident has become rare.

A spectacular accident occurred on Saturday 24th September, 1977, when a low-loader transporting an excavator struck the A68 overbridge, knocking it completely off the abutments. Miraculously, no-one was injured, and no trains were in the section. The span was successfully restored the next day, and the replacement masonry can still be seen today.

Appendix One

Statistics

Records of traffic returns on the branch are available from the first full year of opening until 1933, when the figures from the other stations were combined under Loanhead. The returns for the period after 1933 have not been located.

Livestock figures are not reproduced, as in contrast to the healthy mineral tonnage, the amount carried is very small. For example, in the six months to July 1907, only 20 pigs were recorded at Loanhead, and none from the other stations.

The opening of the extension in 1877 is reflected in the tables, as is the closure of Gilmerton during World War I.

Passengers

	Glencorse	Roslin	Loanhead	Gilmerton	Total	Millerhill
1874	*	*	*	*	*	*
1875	*	7,514	9,128	2,479	19,121	24,698
1876	*	17,336	19,420	4,930	41,686	32,922
1877	*	17,977	21,783	4,975	44,735	33,900
1878	8,467	17,084	24,996	5,186	55,233	33,085
1879	18,795	19,284	31,261	5,611	74,951	34,342
1880	18,860	23,237	27,284	4,760	74,141	32,106
1881	19,019	20,516	31,106	5,313	75,954	34,704
1882	20,267	19,817	36,007	6,064	81,525	38,439
1883	21,163	20,377	39,879	6,181	87,600	40,502
1884	20,797	21,944	43,762	6,219	92,722	38,057
1885	22,807	22,331	46,972	6,469	98,579	36,480
1886	19,538	20,920	43,774	5,658	89,890	32,631
1887	21,526	21,798	43,460	5,439	92,223	32,120
1888	19,945	21,853	40,361	6,156	88,315	32,051
1889	19,730	23,430	45,349	7,544	96,053	30,923
1890	20,104	23,246	44,078	6,834	94,262	31,196
1891	23,096	26,031	47,672	7,445	104,244	32,652
1892	26,510	25,860	50,219	7,266	109,855	37,652
1893	27,569	27,237	52,298	7,830	114,934	34,681
1894	26,565	25,627	49,075	7,478	108,745	32,528
1895	23,097	25,123	44,851	6,394	99,465	33,115
1896	22,477	26,232	48,292	6,610	103,611	33,616
1897	23,917	26,974	47,109	7,338	105,338	33,704
1898	25,714	28,086	42,317	7,176	103,293	33,859
1899	28,261	26,527	36,250	6,765	97,803	33,511
1900	28,943	26,626	39,542	7,767	102,878	33,715
1901	34,618	31,395	41,627	8,242	115,432	35,544
1902	35,444	33,719	45,426	8,058	122,647	36,683
1903	38,173	32,800	49,358	7,433	127,764	35,475
1904	37,670	33,280	55,630	7,332	133,912	34,886
1905	38,700	31,111	56,352	6,900	133,033	34,551
1906	37,169	33,193	64,920	9,596	144,878	32,292
1907	33,717	35,279	65,739	7,318	172,053	32,495
1908	30,678	36,379	31,939	13,605	142,601	35,250
1909	26,617	34,218	56,392	17,676	134,703	34,680
1910	19,561	33,403	51,065	9,017	113,046	32,674

Passengers (continued)

	Glencorse	Roslin	Loanhead	Gilmerton	Total	Millerhill
1911	17,317	34,572	51,713	7,823	111,245	33,218
1912	19,123	36,166	53,546	7,711	116,546	32,260
1913	14,748	34,209	50,548	6,420	105,925	28,800
1914	13,182	41,618	53,862	7,693	116,355	37,503
1915	31,381	32,407	36,894	7,987	108,669	39,277
1916	65,155	38,946	48,039	9,703	161,543	40,595
1917	22,859	11,186	11,968	-	46,013	24,363
1918	14,512	16,119	16,593	-	47,224	31,632
1919	23,140	38,779	39,154	6,431	107,504	43,963
1920	9,084	41,285	39,016	8,856	98,241	54,962
1921	7,921	26,754	25,604	6,299	66,578	43,215
1922	8,220	24,291	27,102	6,281	65,894	44,542
1923	7,472	25,497	3,530	6,730	75,029	50,207
1924	7,850	27,853	34,255	6,726	75,584	54,669
1925	5,307	28,243	30,063	5,963	69,576	55,222
1926	4,409	24,546	21,621	3,873	54,449	41,848
1927	3,897	26,085	25,452	4,250	59,684	38,191
1928	4,048	28,828	24,226	4,057	61,169	32,309
1929	3,284	35,443	27,644	5,096	71,467	37,695
1930	2,244	31,917	28,309	5,088	66,558	31,349
1931	1,685	29,105	27,640	3,427	60,337	27,485
1932	1,184	26,947	27,192	3,022	58,345	27,853
1933	375	7,570	9,912	845	18,702	25,167
1934	-	-	2,826	-	2,826	21,563

Coal in Tons

	Glencorse	Roslin	Loanhead	Gilmerton	Total	Millerhill
1874	*	*	*	*	*	*
1875	*	292	2,056	*	2,348	2,092
1876	*	645	1,980	456	3,081	2,309
1877	*	689	4,952	176	5,817	2,171
1878	522	877	17,046	548	18,993	2,727
1879	1,676	982	16,458	354	19,470	2,436
1880	1,885	834	19,191	311	22,221	2,062
1881	2,454	981	19,320	252	31,007	3,696
1882	2,572	920	21,764	16,049	41,305	3,919
1883	2,702	932	24,583	16,127	44,344	3,453
1884	2,744	1,324	45,828	18,686	68,582	3,671
1885	3,037	1,203	56,618	15,994	76,852	2,941
1886	3,274	913	46,991	18,373	69,551	661
1887	3,751	872	43,734	12,174	60,531	771
1888	7,714	1,705	58,506	16,484	84,409	671
1889	5,399	3,688	72,485	30,382	111,954	528
1890	6,296	1,925	72,558	24,065	104,844	413
1891	7,147	1,016	77,584	20,044	105,791	260
1892	5,094	2,116	83,315	9,902	100,427	265
1893	4,888	1,945	81,295	7,536	95,664	212
1894	4,354	1,120	74,258	22,718	102,450	213
1895	4,581	1,167	51,638	32,883	90,269	208
1896	7,497	1,146	68,958	39,675	117,276	18,173
1897	8,174	958	66,436	32,703	108,271	58,424
1898	6,380	1,218	35,266	23,432	66,296	71,303
1899	5,801	1,064	7,717	1,224	15,806	98,238

Coal in Tons (continued)

	Glencorse	Roslin	Loanhead	Gilmerton	Total	Millerhill
1900	5,473	1,131	11,465	7,331	25,400	96,891
1901	5,300	1,071	6,760	3,533	16,664	103,156
1902	4,870	1,158	5,297	2,300	13,625	98,822
1903	5,260	1,444	6,797	2,250	15,751	111,589
1904	4,884	1,870	6,041	1,825	14,617	121,404
1905	6,123	1,312	4,909	2,708	15,052	143,381
1906	6,018	1,149	5,105	1,212	13,484	168,687
1907	5,515	976	6,173	1,083	13,743	193,872
1908	6,067	912	5,353	2,321	14,653	215,362
1909	5,089	649	4,444	327	10,509	210,734
1910	5,360	760	5,004	669	11,793	293,020
1911	5,725	675	5,975	822	13,197	257,587
1912	4,760	781	6,930	999	13,470	272,062
1913	3,110	548	6,152	759	10,569	234,742
1914	6,680	491	6,314	1,670	15,155	229,028
1915	7,787	563	5,570	1,426	15,346	178,713
1916	8,636	499	6,614	1,933	17,682	182,396
1917	9,322	447	7,348	-	17,117	176,734
1918	7,063	1,071	5,802	-	13,936	188,759
1919	7,719	403	5,727	956	14,805	207,103
1920	6,756	425	8,303	1,474	16,958	221,738
1921	4,631	360	9,892	882	15,765	163,699
1922	7,268	441	8,325	1,709	17,713	251,914
1923	7,596	585	11,359	1,577	21,117	264,552
1924	7,542	425	32,054	1,080	41,101	229,869
1925	8,154	701	35,051	1,228	45,134	258,557
1926	4,893	1,441	32,436	1,234	40,004	175,379
1927	7,509	678	15,747	7,929	31,863	366,710
1928	7,008	714	94,050	5,830	107,602	426,336
1929	4,182	344	109,339	749	114,614	430,896
1930	3,350	381	81,661	561	85,953	466,648
1931	-	-	54,600	-	54,600	548,326
1932	-	-	4,441	-	4,441	340,737

Minerals in Tons

1874	*	*	*	*	*	*
1875	*	1,439	2,019	418	3,876	1,295
1876	*	2,312	2,641	4,374	9,327	563
1877	*	4,839	5,035	4,415	14,289	1,734
1878	1,790	3,191	7,446	3,894	16,321	3,118
1879	1,459	1,779	7,792	3,760	14,790	3,143
1880	1,365	1,776	3,173	4,425	10,739	3,412
1881	1,183	2,073	8,661	3,616	15,543	3,126
1882	1,330	769	5,141	3,354	10,594	5,681
1883	3,198	683	12,583	2,787	19,251	3,879
1884	647	912	11,399	2,704	15,662	3,124
1885	1,348	1,853	9,799	4,518	17,518	4,237
1886	1,548	189	12,703	852	15,292	4,943
1887	740	599	9,061	9,386	19,786	7,187
1888	1,922	580	4,256	3,336	10,094	4,448
1889	1,462	545	6,009	2,809	10,825	5,066

Minerals in Tons (continued)

	Glencorse	Roslin	Loanhead	Gilmerton	Total	Millerhill
1890	1,546	710	4,896	5,076	12,228	4,756
1891	840	771	4,008	2,093	7,712	9,374
1892	1,927	642	7,242	4,808	14,619	22,599
1893	1,668	2,153	10,077	2,651	16,549	19,698
1894	2,713	1,743	8,181	5,316	17,953	3,833
1895	1,815	1,577	10,298	3,279	16,969	2,652
1896	3,003	2,261	7,436	3,300	16,000	29,171
1897	3,416	1,796	6,709	2,309	14,230	59,743
1898	5,917	1,203	18,663	2,184	27,967	26,643
1899	3,313	938	9,011	1,428	14,690	21,288
1900	2,331	1,356	13,370	1,225	20,613	21,996
1901	2,368	1,381	16,279	1,686	21,714	14,860
1902	4,718	1,269	20,954	2,584	29,525	21,097
1903	8,626	2,054	22,961	1,558	35,199	12,120
1904	8,396	770	10,476	2,464	22,106	13,739
1905	5,635	2,267	6,004	2,305	16,211	13,055
1906	3,360	2,539	6,767	2,275	15,441	14,032
1907	6,592	1,458	8,719	2,355	16,124	21,172
1908	2,468	2,838	7,911	2,638	15,855	26,342
1909	2,592	2,532	9,440	2,772	17,336	37,596
1910	2,664	2,691	9,444	3,916	18,715	28,323
1911	2,077	3,399	13,315	5,592	24,383	24,032
1912	2,018	2,991	18,894	2,710	26,613	22,167
1913	2,058	2,246	35,856	5,458	42,618	22,054
1914	3,575	3,914	33,295	1,969	42,753	25,004
1915	2,241	2,377	36,505	1,698	42,821	14,805
1916	2,255	1,213	35,364	1,993	40,825	12,665
1917	3,211	3,544	35,154	-	41,909	16,010
1918	2,996	2,191	25,271	-	30,458	14,475
1919	2,994	1,557	3,424	1,465	9,440	10,386
1920	2,025	1,873	16,443	2,159	22,500	8,660
1921	1,453	869	24,492	2,091	28,905	6,980
1922	895	966	28,851	1,287	31,999	6,965
1923	1,489	961	46,970	997	50,397	7,750
1924	890	1,178	39,705	598	42,371	7,758
1925	1,092	898	17,122	3,231	22,343	7,472
1926	1,140	2,466	21,560	3,130	25,166	2,562
1927	1,150	1,623	22,577	1,475	26,825	4,013
1928	643	2,887	36,668	444	40,662	3,250
1929	1,410	602	18,547	370	20,929	904
1930	874	1,923	29,700	284	32,781	691
1931	469	1,343	33,042	78	34,932	390
1932	*	*	17,089	*	17,089	380
1933	*	*	19,648	*	19,648	149

Goods in Tons

	Glencorse	Roslin	Loanhead	Gilmerton	Total	Millerhill
1874	*	*	*	*	*	*
1875	*	508	2,457	396	3,361	1,817
1876	*	5,606	2,720	1,098	9,424	1,144
1877	*	3,440	5,275	4,415	13,130	1,714
1878	1,178	3,171	4,043	3,894	12,286	1,406
1879	1,870	3,179	4,415	1,665	11,129	2,389

Goods in Tons (continued)

	Glencorse	Roslin	Loanhead	Gilmerton	Total	Millerhill
1880	1,947	2,764	4,868	1,265	10,844	6,788
1881	2,101	3,368	7,666	1,538	14,673	1,390
1882	2,262	2,721	14,612	1,572	21,167	2,567
1883	2,627	2,527	19,969	1,329	26,452	2,276
1884	2,065	1,378	11,399	1,134	15,976	2,270
1885	2,360	1,120	36,268	1,224	40,972	2,038
1886	2,241	997	43,109	511	46,858	1,784
1887	2,201	817	38,347	817	42,182	2,577
1888	2,426	1,073	41,161	1,073	45,733	2,382
1889	2,079	700	50,338	700	53,817	1,947
1890	2,149	797	40,005	533	43,484	1,626
1891	2,717	605	37,964	340	41,626	2,253
1892	3,484	847	37,769	614	42,714	1,344
1893	2,609	713	41,064	623	45,009	2,421
1894	1,486	686	35,783	594	38,549	2,401
1895	1,489	668	25,412	918	28,487	1,619
1896	1,789	627	46,800	977	50,193	1,939
1897	1,661	555	43,478	1,145	46,839	1,506
1898	1,365	724	27,319	903	30,311	1,467
1899	1,309	653	8,968	505	11,435	1,405
1900	1,225	728	7,629	596	10,178	1,441
1901	3,224	731	7,707	701	12,363	1,678
1902	5,027	877	7,981	1,296	15,181	1,746
1903	4,821	1,124	7,505	1,380	14,830	1,768
1904	3,964	1,268	10,060	1,202	16,494	2,202
1905	5,477	1,955	9,017	904	17,353	2,643
1906	1,848	1,877	9,753	807	14,295	2,477
1907	5,628	2,535	9,866	949	18,978	1,909
1908	2,468	2,531	10,205	910	16,114	2,671
1909	2,592	2,452	9,614	985	15,643	2,559
1910	2,664	2,402	9,498	1,054	15,618	3,118
1911	2,077	2,431	9,830	1,042	15,380	3,058
1912	2,018	2,070	12,362	1,460	17,910	2,465
1913	2,058	1,552	9,942	1,356	14,908	2,254
1914	2,276	2,186	7,250	900	12,612	2,906
1915	2,067	1,841	6,373	904	11,185	2,660
1916	2,149	2,158	8,866	851	14,024	1,564
1917	2,594	2,984	10,581	-	16,159	3,346
1918	2,008	2,762	8,899	-	13,669	4,364
1919	1,711	3,953	10,213	742	16,619	2,992
1920	3,557	4,177	11,230	2,272	21,236	2,427
1921	3,018	2,047	7,026	1,398	13,489	2,552
1922	1,219	3,238	6,326	873	11,656	1,415
1923	2,034	3,724	5,919	1,181	12,858	1,959
1924	879	2,765	6,696	770	11,110	1,863
1925	501	2,596	5,744	1,437	10,278	1,582
1926	502	2,231	5,305	1,152	9,190	1,408
1927	576	2,849	8,103	906	12,434	1,194
1928	479	3,007	6,633	1,691	11,810	964
1929	669	3,369	1,701	108	5,847	1,116
1930	483	2,563	1,442	58	4,546	1,825
1931	*	*	1,340	25	1,365	1,856
1932	*	*	1,409		1,409	689

The line to Pentland Oil Works.
Reproduced from the 25", 1896 Ordnance Survey Map

Inset, top left: The west end of the tunnel under the B701 at Straiton has remained forgotten and undisturbed for almost a century, but remains in excellent condition, as can be seen in this view taken in August 1997.   *Author*

Right: The site of the former level crossing at Straiton is now the entrance to a local nature reserve managed by Midlothian Council.
Author

Appendix Two

Straiton Sidings

To the present day motorist driving south from Edinburgh on the A701, the only evidence of the once extensive shale oil and limestone industry which dominated the area is the large kilns, once owned by Bairds the Gartsherrie ironmasters, at Burdiehouse. Similarly, further south, at Straiton, the cottages on the west side of the road give little clue as to their origin, as part of a community of around 150 dwellings which also had its own church.

Shale oil

Shale oil production at Straiton predated the opening of the ELR, as Wm Taylor & Co. of Leith had commenced mining by 1866. The workings were taken over in 1876 by the Straiton Estate Co. Ltd, but financial problems forced the sale once again in 1882, to the Midlothian Oil Company. By this time the plant was in poor order, and had to be rebuilt extensively. The financial position did not improve, however, and three years later, the Clippens Oil Co., based in Paisley, bought over the company.

The Clippens company had been in a similar situation to that of the Shotts Iron Co., namely that the local supply of shale in the West of Scotland had become exhausted, and had sought new sources. In 1881, leases had been taken nearby at Pentland and, by 1882, a large works had been constructed. It retained its Paisley refinery, transporting the oil by rail.

Being the only local producer of shale oil did not protect the company from trouble, natural or financial. A series of fires at the refinery in 1884 and 1885 were followed by strikes by the Pentland workforce in 1886, and severe flooding the following year . The situation was compounded by a rise in the quantity of oil imported from the United States.

New mines were sunk in an attempt to increase production, but the financial situation grew steadily worse, with the liquidator being called in in 1892. Ironically, his report revealed that the company had never been in a better physical condition, and advised financial reconstruction. Accordingly, another new company was formed in 1893 and, despite a coal strike in the following year was able to continue in business. The refinery at Paisley was closed and the refining concentrated at Straiton.

By 1897, things had improved, with 500 miners employed, when a legal situation developed from an unexpected source which led eventually to the demise of the shale oil industry in this part of Midlothian.

As part of the 19th century drive to improve public health, great emphasis was placed on the provision of a public water supply for Edinburgh, with two underground aqueducts bringing water from the south. Both of these passed through the shale field, protected by an act of Parliament which gave water companies the option to buy minerals within 40 yards of the line of their pipes, to prevent subsidence. The Clippens Co. had driven several roads beneath the pipes to access the shale beyond, the water company not having exercised its option to buy in each case. When the Clippens Co. advised that it intended to remove the supporting pillars of shale, the water company obtained an interdict to stop mining near the pipes, which effectively prevented mining altogether.

The existing stock of shale was exhausted by July, causing the refinery to close. After nearly 10 years of legal wrangling the company was finally put into liquidation in 1908, after an unsuccessful attempt to sell the plant and works.

Clippens No. 1, sporting a very North American style spark arrester was, in fact, the second locomotive to carry the number. Photographed when new at Andrew Barclay's works (No. 778 of 1897), it carries a plate on the running board stating 'This locomotive is the property of W.S. Brown Esq. Glasgow'.
Hunslet Barclay Archive, with the permission of the Keeper of the Records of Scotland

Andrew Barclay works photograph of Coltness Iron Co. No. 6, which was to be the final locomotive at Straiton, being transferred to Lanarkshire in November 1961. It was scrapped in 1968.   *Hunslet Barclay Archive, with the permission of the Keeper of the Records of Scotland*

Bairds and Scottish Steel Ltd No. 6, photographed at Straiton in 1952, dated from 1881. The 'Ogee' tank and open cab give it a distinctly old-fashioned look. *F. Jones*

Bairds and Scottish Steel No. 8 is something of a 'mystery locomotive', apparently built at the Shotts Iron Co.'s workshops, from parts 'in stock'. Scrapped around 1958, it appears to be very much out of use when photographed in 1952. *F. Jones*

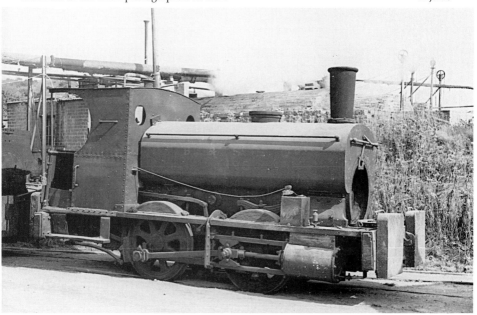

Limestone

The story of limestone production is a happier one, due to the constant demand for lime, as explained in Chapter One.

Having been mined by all of the various oil companies as well as Bairds, the Clippens Oil Co. had inherited all of the pits with its takeover of the Midlothian Oil Co. In 1899, a subsidiary company was formed to run all of the lime production. Even so, by 1921, losses were becoming unsustainable, and the company was sold to the Shotts Iron Co. The formation of the National Coal Board in 1947 did not include industries such as the limeworks, which changed hands yet again, to Bairds and Scottish Steel, a descendant of the original owners of the Burdiehouse kilns.

Closure and the present day

By the late 1950s the limeworks had assumed a semi-derelict air, with rows of wagons quietly rusting in sidings and the locomotive crew having to deal with frequent derailments, due to the parlous state of the track. The steady increase in road traffic also led to longer delays at the level crossing, which had never been equipped with gates sufficiently large enough to close over the entire width of the road.

The closure announcement in 1961 was not surprising, and the works lay undisturbed for a couple of years until late in 1963, when the entire track was relaid with brand new materials, including a loop at Straiton, the earlier system having managed without such a facility. Hopes of the works reopening were short-lived, however, as, apart from a contractor's test train, the track was never used and removed early in 1964.

This really was the 'end of the line', the plant being demolished at the same time. The site lay unused until the 1970s, when a road transport company built its depot next to the main road, using the former rail access as the entrance. At this time parts of the line to Mortonhall pit were still visible, part of the cutting to the north-west of the B702 could be seen, and all of the 'main line' to Straiton Sidings remained, as did the stone level crossing gateposts. The site of Mortonhall pit and the shale pit had disappeared in 1968-9, when the deep holes, which had appeared as the underground workings subsided, had been used as landfill for refuse from Edinburgh. The limekilns and the remains of a small quarry are all that is left, the rest having been returned to farmland. In 1989 a modern Retail Park was built on the site of Straiton limeworks, removing almost all traces of the former use. The Park has recently been extended over the land to the south and south-west, which had remained derelict since the closure. The solum of the 'main line', however, was purchased by Midlothian District Council, to be used as a pedestrian access to the former Straiton Sidings area, now a Nature Reserve. This gives excellent access to this part of the branch and the City bypass bridge. Two other relics of the past are also visible, the first being the arch of the bridge which carried the B702 over the line to Mortonhall pit, and which can still be seen behind the wall on the left, immediately north of the entrance to the Retail Park. Although much overgrown, having been disused for nearly a century, the yellow brickwork is well preserved. The other is a large concrete foundation, whose original purpose may have been to support a crushing plant, mostly hidden by trees, beside the A701, immediately south of Straiton farm. Presumably its size has made removal uneconomic.

The Railway System

The various workings were served by a mineral line which left the branch just north of Loanhead, between Edgefield and Standard sidings. Several loops and sidings were provided for the transfer of traffic, and the line headed south-west on a rising gradient, to cross the B702 Straiton-Loanhead road on the level. A cottage was provided for the gatekeeper and his family. The line then skirted the right-hand side of a bing and a system of sidings fanned out to serve the various parts of the works. The easternmost siding, approached by a steep gradient, originally ran into the Straiton oil works but, latterly, this was used to load the lime kilns.

The 'main line' meanwhile carried on southwards, and after turning through 90 degrees, crossed the Straiton-Penicuik road (A701) on the level and entered the Pentland oil works.

The pits and limeworks at Burdiehouse were rail connected, by a line which also took in the Straiton lime works. It then entered a wooded cutting and passed under the B702, by the bridge already described, continuing in a shallow cutting for 250 yards before branching to reach the shale pit. Mortonhall pit and Burdiehouse limeworks were at the easternmost end of the line, a ¼ mile further on.

As with the majority of Scottish Industries which had a railway system, Straiton used a total of six 0-4-0 saddle tank locomotives during its existence, four of which were supplied by Andrew Barclay & Co., of Kilmarnock. An engine shed was provided, but was capable of holding one locomotive only. No.1, Barclay Works No. 193, was supplied in 1878, presumably for the opening of the works, and lasted until the takeover by the Shotts Iron Co. in 1921, when it was transferred to its Lanarkshire Ironworks. It was scrapped in 1960 by the National Coal Board.

A second locomotive was required by the 1890s, and another Barclay product, No. 778 of 1897, arrived fully lined out, curiously (as it was the second engine) also numbered 1, and even more intriguing, fitted with a form of spark arresting chimney, which gave it a distinctly North American look. The financial state of the company was however reflected by the cast notice fixed to the running plate, which stated that 'This locomotive is the property of W.S. Brown Esq., Glasgow', one of the Directors of the Clippens Co. It was sold to the Glasgow Iron Co. at an unknown date, and scrapped in 1955.

The 1921 takeover resulted in locomotives being transferred and/or rebuilt by the Shotts company. Little is known of the first engine to arrive at Straiton under the new management, other than that it carried the number 10 and the name *Drumpellier*, the name of a colliery and ironworks in Coatbridge. Exactly how long it was employed at Straiton, or its eventual fate, is unknown.

The year 1947 saw the next transfers, with two locomotives arriving, Nos. 6 and 8. No. 6 (makers' No. 282) had been built at the Riverbank works, Kilmarnock in 1881 by Barclays & Co. This was an independent concern started in 1869 and financed by Andrew Barclay, with his younger brother, John, in charge. No. 6 had been delivered new to a Wishaw firm rejoicing in the name of the Belhaven Iron, Steel & Patent Nail Co. Ltd., and had been acquired by Bairds & Scottish Steel in the 1920s. It lasted only until 1956, when it was sent to Connell, Coatbridge for scrapping.

No. 8 is also something of a mystery locomotive, built apparently by the SIC at an unknown date, and scrapped around 1958. It certainly appears to have been out of use when photographed in 1952.

With the demise of No. 6, a replacement was necessary, and another Andrew Barclay locomotive, also No. 6, was aquired from the Coltness Iron Co. of Newmains, near Wishaw. The new No. 6 (Works No. 1508 of 1918) was destined to have a short working life at Stration, lasting until the closure in November 1961. Transferred back to Lanarkshire, this time to Bairds' Northburn works at Kipps, Coatbridge, it was eventually scrapped in 1968.

Appendix Three

Report by James Bell, NBR Engineer

In the following report, the NBR Engineer reflects the Victorian concern with public hygiene, when he recommends improvements to the facilities at Gilmerton. His remark concerning the 'expense of maintenance' in connection with the Loanhead goods shed is ironic, as it still stands, some 125 years later.

North British Railway Company
Engineers Office
Edinburgh 29th Dec. 1873

To: L.Mason Esq.
General Manager.

Dear Sir,

Millerhill & Rosslyn Railway

Your letter of 19th inst.
I walked over the Millerhill and Rosslyn Railway, as far as Loanhead Station, on 25th inst. and beg to make the following Report as to the state of the Works:

Bridges under line

There are five Underbridges - two of 36 feet, two of 12 feet, and one of 8 feet span. The abutments and wing walls are built of square block masonry with mallable iron beams and timber cladding. Two of the bridges carry the Railway over the Turnpike road to Dalkeith, one over the road to Drum Farm, and two over cattle paths.
The above bridges are in good order.

Bridges over line

There are five Overbridges. Four of them are built of square block masonry in the abutments and wing walls with cast iron beams and parapets, having a brick arch between the beams to carry the roadway. The other bridge is of square block masonry in abutments and wing walls, with brick arch.
The above bridges are in good order.

Culverts

There is one culvert of three feet span - the abutments and wing walls are of square block rubble work, with a brick arch. With the exception of pitching which is required for the water course, the above is in good order.

Fences

The line is fenced with a seven wire fence, with posts placed 6 feet apart, all of which are in good order.

Field Crossings

There are five field crossings all furnished with iron gates - locks are required for these.

Alterations on roads

Fence walls to the extent of the road alterations, require to be built from the parapets of the bridges. The whole of the roads require a substantial coat of whinstone metal.

Cuttings

Walls require to be built above the foot of the slopes in Gilmerton cutting to retain the stuff [*sic*]. The side drains also require to be deepened to allow the water to get off.

Ballast

The ballast in general is composed of hard burnt ashes. With the exception of the soft freestone ballast in Gilmerton cutting, which should be removed, it is quite satisfactory.

Sleepers

The sleepers are of Baltic Timber, uncreosoted, and average 9 feet long and 10 inches broad, the average lifetime of which will not exceed five years.

Rails &c.

The rails are in 24 feet lengths, and weigh 75lb. per linear yard. They are fastened at the joints with the usual suspended fish - the chairs weigh 32 lb. each - there are 8 sleepers under each rail, and the chairs are fastened to them with two mallable iron spikes ⅞ in. diam. each. The rails are fastened in the chairs with oak keys made to fit tight into them.

State of the line

The Line in general is in good order, but it will be necessary to give some portions a good lift, and adjust the rails before the North British engines pass over it.

Gilmerton Station

This station consists of an Agent's house, Booking Office, Waiting Room and Passenger Shed with W.C. and Urinals. The painting and other furnishings are in hand. A 3 ton

Loading Bank Crane and a Cart Steelyard are required for the Goods yard. There is no Goods Shed or Lamp Room. Lamps are required for the Passenger Shed and Platform. There is no supply of water to this Station, the want of which is very much felt. The Water Closets are on the dry pan system - a good supply of water should be brought in and the W.C. furnished with patent pan apparatus and connected to a 9 in. spigot and faucet pipe drain - this will enable the W.C.to be properly flushed.

It will be necessary to alter and adjust the siding to allow the heavy engines to work with more freedom over them. Catch points are also required for the siding.

Loanhead Station

This station consists of a Booking Office, Waiting Room, and Passenger Shed, with W.C. and Urinals, and Goods Shed. The painting and furnishing are in hand. An Agent's house is much required at this station. A 3 ton Loading Bank Crane, and Cart Steelyard are required for the goods yard, and a 30 cwt. Crane for the Goods Shed. Lamps are required for the Platform and Passenger Shed.

The Sidings require to be altered and adjusted before heavy engines can work over them with freedom - catch points are also required.

Signals

With the exception of Millerhill Junction, no signals have been erected on this railway.

Yours Truly,

James Bell.

Note of requirements for the Loanhead and Roslin Railway

Gilmerton

Clock for Station
  do. for Signal Box
Alter name plates on signal levers from 'Down' line to 'Up' line and from 'Up' line to 'Down' line.

Up distant signal has a very bad background, as seen from the Signal Box: it ought either to be carried 100 to 200 yards further out, or be raised about 10 feet.

Down distant signal is not far enough out from the first fouling point: should be distant therefrom at least 800 yards: instead of cutting the trees down recommend that the signal be carried out to the first underbridge.

Edgefield and Quarry Sidings

Catch point of Quarry siding on wrong side of line and too near main line: should be carried back 20 yards and run into face of bank. Shift siding signal back accordingly. The space between Signal Cabin and bridge at Edgefield requires to be fenced.
Clock for Signal Box.

Loanhead

Indicator wanted for Up Loop points.
Land bought for station master's house but no house built.
Wooden Goods Shed - adds to the expense of maintenance.
Waiting Room requires furniture.
Clock for Station and for Signal Box.
Loop line signals to be made to work to 'danger' and 'caution' and a semaphore signal wanted for south end of loop.

Boroughlee

Clock for Signal Box.
The Down distant signal should have been from 5 to 10 feet higher - this siding is signalled from one direction as a junction, and from the other as a siding.
Drivers do not get a good view of the Up distant signal, it being too low.

Roslin

Clocks wanted for Station and Signal Cabin.
The fencing on various parts of the line requires to be seen to, as there are one or two open spaces on it, which might admit livestock on the line.

Note of Staff

Gilmerton	-	1 Agent, 1 Signalman	20s.
Edgefield	-	1 Signalman	20s.
Loanhead	-	1 Agent, 1 Signalman	20s.
		1 Porter	17s. 6d.
Boroughlee	-	1 Signalman	20s.
Roslin	-	1 Agent, £60 p.a.	
		1 Porter	17s. 6d.
		1 Signalman	20s.

Note: Probably a Lampman will be required for Edgefield, Loanhead and Boroughlee, at 19s. Millerhill also requires a Lampman, at 19s.

Bibliography

The following documents are held by the Scottish Record Office:

Minute books of the Edinburgh, Loanhead and Roslin Railway, ref. BR/EDL
NBR Minute books and Secretary's letter books
NBR Working Timetables, ref. BR/TT(S)/52
NBR Sidings registers, ref. NBR/4/385. etc.
NBR Viaduct Replacement Report, ref. BR/NBR/4/386
NBR Station Takings books
LNER Working Timetables ref. BR/TT(S)/50
LNER Closure Notice, ref. BR/LNE/8/325
Bouch's papers, ref. GD266

The North British Railway Vols. 1 & 2, John Thomas, David & Charles (1971)
North British Railway Album, A.A. McLean, Ian Allan (1975)
The Story of Shotts, A. Muir, The Shotts Iron Co. Ltd (1946)
Mining in Mid and East Lothian, A.S. Cunningham (1925)
The Limestones of Scotland, HMSO, 1948 (Reprinted 1976)
Rosslyn - Its Castle, Chapel and Scenic Lore, Will Grant, Macniven & Walker, Edinburgh (1947)
Forgotten Railways: Southern Scotland, John Thomas, David & Charles
British Railways Marshalling Yards, Michael Rhodes, Oxford Publishing Co.
Handbook S - Scotland, The Industrial Railway Society (1976)
Barclay 150, Russell Wear, Hunslet-Barclay Ltd (1990)
'The Shale Oil Industry at Pentland and Straiton, Midlothian', David Kerr, *Scottish Local History Journal* Vol. 37 June 1996
Bradshaw's Railway Manual (1877)
The Annals of Penicuick, J.J. Wilson (1891)
The Origins of the Scottish Railway System 1722-1844, C.J.A. Robertson, John Donald (1893)
Locomotives of the LNER (Various Vols.), Railway, Correspondence & Travel Society.

In addition, the free access granted by members of the North British Study Group to papers in their private collections is gratefully acknowledged.

The works plate from Bilston Glen shunter No. 32, now in the Author's collection.

Author